ANCHOR BOOKS

THE NHS EXPERIENCE

Edited by

Suzy Goodall

First published in Great Britain in 1996 by
ANCHOR BOOKS
1-2 Wainman Road, Woodston,
Peterborough, PE2 7BU

HB ISBN 1 85930 495 8
SB ISBN 1 85930 490 7

Foreword

Anchor Books is a small press, established in 1992, with the aim of promoting readable poetry to as wide an audience as possible.

We hope to establish an outlet for writers of poetry who may have struggled to see their work in print.

The poems presented here have been selected from many entries. Editing proved to be a difficult and daunting task and as the Editor, the final selection was mine.

At some time in our lives we may experience the National Health Service, being it going to the doctor's, hospital or dentist. Have you spent time in hospital? How did you feel? How do you feel about all the things that are going on in the NHS at the moment.

The poets included in this book, give the reader a wonderful insight into their thoughts and experiences of the NHS. Nurses, doctors and patients all unite together to make this book a joy to read by all.

I trust this selection will delight and please the authors and all those who enjoy reading poetry.

Suzy Goodall
Editor

CONTENTS

DOCTOR DOCTOR

Doctor doctor, tell us true
Because we don't know what to do.
Have we only months to live?
That's our life you're playing with
Your time is precious we all know,
As on your rounds you cheerfully go.
Dishing out the pills and potions
Telling nurse to rub on lotions,
Prodding here, squeezing there,
Giving our feelings little care,
Jabbing needles, X-rays, shaking head,
While we lie quaking on the bed,
Now you have got us in a lather,
When at bed foot you have a blather
Then smiling say, can do no more here
You can go home tomorrow dear!
Does that mean that we are cured
Or should we check that we're insured.

George Bailey

COUNTRY NURSE

Now morning has come and the rush begins
The District Nurse should really have wings
For the busy traffic during the rush hour
Knowledge of quick routes their only power
Now using the modern day motor car
They can visit more patients and travel far
And the push-bike is no longer seen
But would it be useful in the city-scene?
Not practical though on the country farms
Carrying bandages, dressings in their arms
Those bumpy lanes, full of puddles
Lost in a village, signposts in a muddle
With the black bag and obvious uniform
Helping the patients and relatives conform
To relieve anxiety and ease their pain
And teach them how to cope again
Nurses reassure them they are not alone
And aim to assist 'The Sick' in their home.

Susan Gerry

HOSPITAL

Hospital . . . I didn't like it!
Being ill, in hospital . . . I didn't like it!
Driving, to the hospital . . . I didn't like it!
Visiting someone, in hospital . . . I didn't like it!

Having an operation, in hospital . . . I didn't like it!
Recovering after an accident, in hospital . . . I didn't like it!
My wife, being in hospital . . . I didn't like it!
My daughter, being in hospital . . . I didn't like it!

My dad was in hospital . . . I didn't like it!
My Grandad was, in hospital, then he died, in hospital . . . I didn't like it!
A friend was in hospital . . . I didn't like it!
My wife had my baby daughter, in hospital . . . I didn't like it!
(The hospital, not the baby!)

That odious smell of disinfectant in hospital . . . I don't like it!
The shiny floors that make your shoes squeak, in hospital . . . I don't like it!
Extortionate car park rates, at hospitals . . . I don't like it!
To be perfectly honest . . . I don't like hospitals, but,
may we thank God for the doctors and nurses who work
in hospitals even if I don't like them, (the hospitals that is),

The work they do is second only to God himself,
couldn't we have nurses in libraries or something?
Did I say I don't like hospitals?

Ron Matthews Jr

THE NHS PATIENT

Maisie lay on a hospital trolley
Waiting for doctor, and feeling a wally
She was parked in a corridor, with only a sheet
To cover her nakedness, and keep in the heat

A white-coated figure came passing by
He lifted her sheet, and gazed with a sigh
'This pain' said Maisie, 'just what is the cause?'
He said, 'Don't ask me, I'm painting the doors!'

Margaret Sanderson

THE CRISPLY STARCHED CAP

I stayed in hospitals on a few occasions
To have a baby, some tests and two operations.
53 years ago, the first time was grim
You could tell the place a workhouse had been.
As it was wartime there wasn't much food
And what they gave us wasn't much good
We brought our own rations which soon disappeared
And waited for visitors to bring us a treat.
But the nursing was splendid for the nurses lived in fear
Of a summons, in front of matron to appear.
This matriarch came morning and night,
In her crisply starched cap, to give us a fright
She stood at the foot of each bed and said:
(In a very stern voice that made us afraid)
'How are you today? You look quite well
Enough to get up and move about for a spell'
We stammered in answer 'Thank you Matron' and she was gone
To the next patient for the same carry on.
Another hospital, many years later.
The building was newer, the food much better
The wards full of flowers, the nurses just fab
There was a stern matron with a crisply starched cap.
I was not there long but I enjoyed my stay
And was almost sorry when I went away.
The next time I was in for an operation
It really wasn't a brilliant occasion
The matron had gone, there was no starched cap
No supervision, the nurses in a flap
The 'Manager', no nurse, was a very young man
Who had no idea how a place for sick people was run.

Lisa Wolfe

THERE'S ONE IN EVERY WARD

In my hospital bed I doze, weary after a night of pain
The peace is shattered by a loud 'UFF', there it goes again.
May as well sit up and see who else there is in here.
A sympathetic smile aimed at the 'UFF' lady. 'I'm really in agony dear.'
They'll have to do something soon I cannot stand much more.
I really shouldn't be in here, I was in Stepping Hill before.
Ah! Here's a nurse she'll see to things'
It's amazing how many 'UFF's' that brings!
'Put the fan on, pass my puffer, my asthma's bad today.
I've a migraine coming on' then more 'UFF's' come into play
I dare to ask how did it happen? 'I fell over the cat,
she's clever you know, walks round the room without touching the floor'
The mind boggles - could there be more?
Anxious relatives appear 'See the doctor, see the nurse,
find out what they are going to do. And get me some chocolate
will you love, just you pass me purse
My IBS is coming on, good meals in here are very few.
I will be glad when it's 7 o'clock, then the pills are due'
Night time comes, time for sleep
Then what happens, I feel I could weep?
The light is on till 3am, paper rustles, there's a draught from the fan
Then a loud 'pop' - she's opening a can!
Dawn is breaking is it peace at last?
'UFF' nurse, bring the bedpan, you're going to have to be fast.
Sorry dear, nothing doing, I'll have to wait till morn.
I try so hard to be no trouble, I wish I'd never been born.'

Miki Monnington

THE OPERATION - ODE TO A MR!

On a bright day in June she first met this Mister.
One look at her tum made him sigh then - 'Oh Sister.'
So - beguiled, when he smiled she agreed to his terms
When he promised to rid her of all of them germs.
For she came all a'tremble a'feared and a'fright
Never guessing she'd find such a gallant 'white' knight.
'There's nothing to fear - you're here in our care
One week with us here and you'll be walking on air!'
With a grin and a laugh he bemuses, bewitches -
The next thing she knows he's got her in stitches!
'I'm cut up about it' she told him next day
I don't mind the Dr but what about Mr Fay.
Oh Mr Fay what a Toby you are
If I'd known what was coming I'd been back in the car!
So deftly was done all the cutting and splicing
Not quite sure who did all this 'feather-stitch icing!
Her fate's with them all the Doctors and Nurses
Take no notice of moans, her groans and her curses
She's really enjoyed the company she's in
To have missed it would surely be a 'cardinal sin'!
As she struggles to stand with an 'oh' and an 'aah'
And finds that she really cannot go that great far;
As for doing the splits it's really not on -
She might try a bit later when 'stitches' are gone.
As fit as a fiddle she surely will be
Once she gets over this little lark and a spree.
So although it's OK and she knows he's 'au fait'
'Fraid come what may - it's 'Goodbye' to Fay.
Many thanks for your skill your kindness and care
This Mundesley Moll will remember you there!'

Mollie D Earl

LIFE SAVERS

There's a new 'Technician' in Luton town
Ready to do her bit.
For all mankind be they young or old
She'll be there with her kit.

She passed her exams with flying colours
And knows her Highway Code.
So if she's behind you ringing her bell
Please pull to the side of the road.

Broken limbs or heart attacks
Whatever it may be.
She'll treat you with real kindness
And plenty of sympathy.

Who is the 'Angel' who's joined the ranks
On our ambulances so white.
Theresa is her Christian name
And she'll help you in your plight.

I am *so very proud* of her
She is my daughter you know
And I'd like to tell her in this rhyme
I truly love her so.

Keep up the good work Theresa
And in no time you will see.
With your dedication and determination
a 'Paramedic' you will be.

Thank God for the NH Service
We do not count the cost.
(Private health bills would be sky high)
So, without it, we'd all be lost.

Tricia John

HANGING AROUND

Bending down to stroke the cat
Crack! A disc slipped in my back.
The doc was sent for he looked grave
He pulled and pushed. How I raved.

The hospital I had to go straightaway,
Saw the consultant the same day,
This is severe, he said, you need action
He put me in bed, for a month on traction.

Your feet in the air, your head hanging down,
Dignity, what's that, the nurse said with a frown,
Feet sticking out of the bed covers.
A weight, either side of your leg hovers.

Staring at the ceiling nothing to do.
Rang for the nurse, 'I need you.'
'Just a minute dearie,' she said,
'I've got to make up this other bed.'

Laid for an hour, no-one came,
Amused myself playing an imaginary game,
Found myself in a tangle, one weight slipped
My left foot, over the bedhead it dipped.

Rang the bell, the nurse said what now!
Taken aback, nothing I said with head bowed.
Laying there, one foot turned right,
Put my head under the covers crying with fright.

After four hours, I said this will not do
Nurse I shouted I need the loo
Oh dear said she, you are in a mess
In a tone of voice, she couldn't care less.

I did my month under stress
That was one, encounter with the NHS.

Blanche Middleton

NHS AMANIA

All appeared to be quiet
As tho' the storm had passed
Coming was the morning light
With patients all aghast

I had been whisked to hospital
Under NHS without question
My situation being somewhat vital
Appearing to cause some sensation

Hospital NHS I never before used
Prefer not to sample same again
Patients are inadvertently abused
And they all feel the pain

'Twas like Piccadilly Circus at night
Nurses commuting like 'army patrols'
Rattling commodes with all their might
Everything seeming out of control

I grant respect to every nurse
But some seem not trained enough
Causing patients to feel worse
Plodded with needles and treated rough

I suffered a heart problem
My blood they did thin
A sister roughly my arm injected
Causing pain bruising and bleeding

There was noise thro' the night
Often clamping and banging
One could not possibly sleep tight
There was space for improved hygiene.

Josephine Foreman

THE NATIONAL WEALTH SERVICE

In at the deep end, and not so wealthy,
The National Health Service, is not looking so healthy,
Shortage of beds, means patients start to suffer,
If there is no room at one hospital, they are then sent to another.

Waiting lists growing day by day,
'You will have to wait six months,' they turn to you and say.
By the time you get to see someone, the problem's three times worse
than before,
'There is no bed to admit you now, nice to see you please close the door.'

If you are a private patient, it is a different tune,
You get a letter within 3 days, saying, 'Your appointment will be soon,'
This two tier system, puts people in a stew,
Because they know a private patient, has just gone and jumped the queue.

Overworked, and underpaid,
Staff pay rises, get delayed.
Health Service staff, feel they get a raw deal,
But in order, to keep their jobs, they know they must not squeal.

Devotion to the patients, then becomes so hard to do,
Serving them a sandwich, saying, 'This is all we have for you,'
Emptying a bedpan, typing up a letter,
Sticking the thermometer in the patient's mouth, saying 'I hope you are feeling better?'

101 jobs to do, the bedside manner's gone,
Staff are then so shattered, they cannot carry on,
Management then wonder why, when staff say 'They want to finish,'
If this Government doesn't step in soon the National Health Service will diminish.

Barbara Holme

THE GERM

The Doctor looked quite worried, he shook his furrowed brow,
'I can't tell yet what's caused it, you'll have to have tests now.'
I felt all hot and sticky and came out in big spots,
My skin began to wrinkle, my stomach tied in knots.
My eyes were crossed and squinting, my ears began to twitch,
My hair stood up on all spiky, my nose began to itch.
Students tried to sympathise (they had a lot to learn),
For I had just been smitten with a brand new kind of germ.
Defying medication, old tablets would not do,
They tried hot baths; inhalers; and pills for Asian 'Flu.
The Germ fought back triumphant as I began to sneeze,
One moment I was boiling hot, the next I'd start to freeze.
Then Staff Nurse came to see me, she shook her head with glee,
'I'll sort you out' she chuckled 'tough cases come to me.'
The screens were drawn around me as she pulled on gloves of rubber,
She'd tubes and soapy water, I began to blubber.
Not prudent now to linger - the cure it was too bad,
I left the ward so rapidly, (the students were quite sad).
Yet another patient gone, they'd had no chance to learn
About the antibodies to zap my vicious germ.

But accolades were waiting, when all was done and said,
They'd met NHS targets by emptying another bed!

Drew Michaels

OLD ARTHUR

It was the year nineteen seventy-four
When from my profession I retired.
Some voluntary service I was looking for
And by psychiatry I was inspired.
St Clements Hospital in Ipswich seemed to be the place
Which would offer me an ample scope.
My first day's duties I had to face
And in the helping of patients I had hope.
It was in Warren House that I made my début
And my first patient contact I was shown,
A bewildered old fellow came into view
He would be mine and mine alone.
Old Arthur soon gave me 'Guv'nor' as name,
I soon learned the cause of his fears.
With a story of pigs he to me came
His eyes were flooded with tears.
His pets, he believed, would never be fed
If he wasn't there by their side.
My reassuring words were quickly said
And with thankfulness he cried.
Week after week I saw Arthur, and he
Always looked to me as a friend.
I'd no idea what a shock it would be
When our relationship came to an end.
The poor old fellow had passed away
Quite peacefully in his bed.
From the hospital there that day
Went a poor saddened helper named Fred.

F R Paulsen

THE SPECIAL UNIT

I worked in a bed-finding unit
Which existed for sixty years or so,
But alas, in the year nineteen seventy
With cut-backs . . . this service had to go.

The unit consisted of six members of staff
Who manned emergency phones round-the-clock,
The aim . . . to get people into hospital
To liaise and collaborate with the doc . . .

As, when a doctor was at an emergency
After dealing with the patient and all,
He'd phone to give us information
Then we'd take over as a result of that call.

The first stage was to phone the nearest hospital
To 'Book a bed' for the patient right away,
We'd a direct-line to the ambulance controller
So an *immediate wagon* was soon on its way.

Meanwhile the doctor could continue
To visit more patients and use his valuable time,
And leave us to deal with the practicalities,
To *axe* the special unit was a cost-cutting crime!

We were housed in the City Chamber's Complex
At 23, Montrose Street, to be more specific,
While the Board Management were totally indifferent
The camaraderie within the team was terrific.

A National Health Service is no longer the aim . . .
In fact . . . 'Health is our Business' the new adverts proclaim,
No longer called a patient . . . a client's the new name,
Oh, where is the NHS of international acclaim?

Mary A Scott

UNCONDITIONAL LOVE

The NHS is made
from Beveridge and Bevan bade
political divisions fade
with unconditional love.

The NHS is seized
with medical expertise
to work against disease
with unconditional love.

The NHS is poorly
a sick dogmatic story
some nurses and doctors worry
about unconditional love.

The NHS is dead
starved, martyred and bled
privatised and shed
of its unconditional love.

Margaret Graham

JOBS FOR THE BOYS

The majority of people in Britain
Were happy with their NHS
It was always there when needed
No one turned away - open access.

Then a think tank started a rumour
Like Topsy it just grew and grew
They talk about waiting lists and old buildings
Planting doubts in our minds - is it all true?

PR men thought up a slogan
'The NHS is safe in our hands'
Privatisation - perish the thought!
Just better management you understand!

Close wards to make room for computers
Sumptuous offices and uniformed staff.
Massive perks for accountants and chairmen
Hotel style reception areas - what a laugh!

The massive expense of the NHS goes on
To pay huge salaries, and hard and soft ware
Crumbs left from the cake must be shared
Between 'customers' (users), treatment and care.

Famous hospitals like Barts and Christies
Let's bring them down a peg or two
Privatise them - no one will notice!
Make them available to the chosen few!

Why not open 'do it yourself' theatres
Relatives operating - in service trained
Sell oxygen masks, charge for the loo . . . then . . .
Go the whole hog - buy a Goya or two!

Have things gone too far now - too late for return
To common sense and wide choices?
When family doctors had time to listen
And hospitals were run by medical voices.

Evelyn Dann

NHS CATASTROPHE

The NHS has been there for many years
the family doctor in the NHS is under
threat and so is society. Reflecting
upon the past I remember there were
only four doctors running the practice
now time has changed I see more
and more doctors in one practice alone.
This radical outlook could cause
Catastrophe with people's lives
for the young doctors their
tasks are impossible, with concern
many patients wait, due to the
consequences of time, which is
valuable towards what the doctors
read, and consider their actions
with minutes of their time.

However many people are turning
private towards BUPA, why! I
Say! Is this because, they can
not get whatever medication they
had four months ago in the NHS.
Or is it they may need more time
with the doctor, than what we receive
in the NHS.

Monica R Rehill

GOOD NEWS

Now to the hospital I must go
I've dropped a hammer on my toe,
The swelling's not too bad it's true
Although my foot is turning blue.

I limp along to casualty
The desk clerk says now let me see,
I'll book you in for an X-Ray
You should be called some time today!

I wait and wait and then I doze
To wake up looking at my toes
My name is called and 'goodness me'
The blueness now has reached my knee!

I'm then wheeled off to rooms afar
Where thirteen doctors 'Um' and 'Ahh'
They disappear for their debate
So, once again I wait and wait.

The diagnosis is not good
The leg could poison all my blood
So now, resigned unto my fate,
I know they'll have to amputate.

When I awake from surgery
There's space where my 'good leg' should be
'Get over here' I shout and cough,
You've gone and chopped the wrong one off!

The doctor says 'Now listen to me'
It's only off above the knee
There's good news in the specialist's letter
It says your bad leg's getting better.

J W Whitehead

INTO DAWN

The ambulance will always call again.
That early morning nearly three years gone
The three of us set out on jolting roads -
My futile self, my wife, our unborn son
Whose coming was uncertain as a cord
On which all life's immensities depend -
Set out on dreadful travel into dawn
Where trolleys waited, all the abstract sense,
The clinical appurtenance to love
In centuries of miracle and birth.
And loving mouths more loving under masks
And rubbered hands more gentle than the skin,
Cubicular, compartmented, made man
Of what had seemed mere hopelessness within.

And if he seemed miraculous, that smile
With words and mighty shoulders of man
At two years old could drag me back to birth
With superstitious terror or, perhaps,
Prediction of this blank paralysis
As, years come round, I yield him back to hands
More capable than these of loving acts,
Hands that revived a marvel past despair -
As this is now that goes out to their care.

Alasdair Aston

SMILE PLEASE

It's been a wait but now it's time
To take my case and join the line
There must be ten all look like me
Big fat belly resting on their knee
Name and number taken down by nurse
Feel like a nobody - the NHS curse
Upon my bed I wait some more
Constantly looking towards the door
Afraid of what they will do to me
Too scared to say 'just let me be'
A baby's birth is awaiting us
Hope it's not spoilt by NHS cuts
Just hold my hand give kindly smile
Please help me through just for a while
I moan and groan then lay in wait
Where is my baby this is the date
Then all too soon it seems it's here
Just when the pain's too much to bear
Still no smile on doctor's face
Off out the room at fastest pace
Not even life as new as this
Can gain a cheer from the NHS.

Julie Brumpton

NHS

The NHS is in such a mess
Since the government tried to
run it as a business
But don't blame the doctors
and nurses though
For without the NHS
where would we go.

Waiting lists a mile long
It seems the system's gone
all wrong
Closing hospitals here and there
It makes you wonder whether
the government does care

But thanks to the dedicated
Doctors and nurses who do a
great job and are rushed off
their feet trying to help the
ordinary man in the street.

Janis Pearson

METHODS IN OUR CARING

Caring for the sick as I
  lay there on a drip
The doctor was on his
  rounds much earlier on.
The nurse came to
  change my fluid and fill in
a chart, she has a good heart.
  I came round from my
sleep. The ward was filled
  with beds and people.
Some have visitors there,
  others lie still or stare.
Could anyone imagine a
  bright hot day, serving a hospital
stay. Outside cars come and
  go, staff walk about, and babies shout
Do you wear a blue dress
  or a white coat.
Sickness and cure, the
  bedside water so pure.

Joseph Sagina

TEN, NINE, EIGHT

I thought NHS stood for:
Never Have Sweets
but as a nine year old I was proved wrong
when my leg needed technical adjustment
I thought it would be fun
A few weeks off school
Wasn't I a fool!

They took me to the theatre
Then the importance hit me
I wanted to run but I can't even walk
Surrounded by men in green
I wanted to scream but no,
it was too late
I was counting backwards in my head
Ten, nine, eight
just as I was told
A man came out on a trolley
He looked so old
and all I could think as I was injected to sleep
Was he just nine years old when he went in?

A J Hayward

A HOSPITAL CORRIDOR

A vast expanse of gleaming tiles
span into the distance with style,
walkways dazzling the eye
reflecting the passer-by,
legions pass an ever open door,
footsteps echoing across the floor,
an army of carers walk their beat
constant patter, incessant feet,
wheels glide along with a grace and ease
conveying precious cargo with expertise,
stillness pervades the witching hour
as in the dimness shadows glower
reaching onward toward dawn
feeble the shafts that herald morn.

Sheelagh Evans

WORKING IN THE NATIONAL HEALTH SERVICE

It certainly is not so that you can amass plenty of wealth,
That nurses choose to remain in the National Health
But rather that they may for the majority care,
Without lay persons for ever being there.

After training it is true,
There are several options open to you.
But unless you keep in touch with all the grass roots,
You may soon find yourself sprouting rusty shoots.

The choice of bedside nursing was mine,
Not very lucrative but it suited me fine.
I did try others but soon became aware,
That the National Health Service was where one could really care.

Towards the end of my career, there came a day,
I moved from ward to department - and there I did stay.
For you see ward work can be quite heavy,
And for something lighter I found I was ready.

Some senior nurses their displeasure did show,
And over the grapevine I got to know.
Usually by action or expression of face,
So - you've guessed it - their presence I'd choose not to grace.

A few months later there was a change,
Our sister retired so we had to get used to someone strange.
But I wasn't prepared when I got a reprimand,
For what to me, had not even been a command.

Don't get me wrong - I'd been reproved many times before,
But not in front of a hundred people or more.
I said not one word but shot her a look of disgust.
And ever after that - her treatment was just.

Betty Green

IGNOMINY

I've clambered my way up the corporate ladder,
to acting deputy head.
Success indeed, but I couldn't be sadder
I've caught an infection of the bladder
and spent all week in a hospital bed.
My status has suffered a brutal retreat,
I'm prodded and poked like a piece of old meat,
another statistic, another to treat
amongst hundreds of 'not quite yet dead'.
I suppose I am lucky and shouldn't complain
but the nurses behave like I've lost half my brain
and that's harder to take than the worry and pain.
Next time I'll go private instead.

M P Brown

UNDER PAID PROFESSIONALS

To work hard day and night,
Making sure people are alright,
Changing their beds,
Keeping them clean,
The least of our work,
Most of which is unseen,
But we know about hygiene,
Hard work is what we do,
So that the doctors and nurses can help you,
Some of us are slack we agree,
But we do help,
Making sick healthy,
The domestic, hard work for little money.

Paul Waldock

WAITING!

Sitting, waiting, in a chair,
Was rather more than I could bear!

The patients went down - one by one,
Their operation to be done -
(It seemed my turn would never come)

The clock ticked by,
And there was I,

Still sitting, waiting, in that chair!

My eyes did to the ceiling stare,
As patiently I still sat there.

Two hours went by,
I heaved a sigh,
Every minute wasted, hating,
Hoping for my name to hear -
'Tis nearly my turn - never fear!

Oh!, How I wished me on my way
T'were better ways to pass a day,
Than sitting, waiting, here to-day!

I'd rather be back home alone
Counting blessings -
Not to moan.

Ah! my name is called at last
The 'Waiting game' -
It now has passed.

Freda F Ringrose

GOD IS WITH ME AS WELL

I have suffered many anguishes in my small but short life
Medical problems that have hit me that seem to hurt me,
Eyes of blue that were hit by acute glaucoma,
Leaving me no option but operations to help them.

I was blind after each eye op, a frightening experience,
A fear that inbuilt in me that made me think as well,
Suffering Menieres disease, an ear complaint as well,
I began to think, would I end up, blind, deaf, and unable to
write as well.

Then without a question my hands began to hurt,
Carpal Tunnel an infliction, that hurts me as well,
Three things that hurt me, three consultants that help me,
The NHS behind it, they help me as well.

Now I am suffering headaches, deep inside my head,
When will these problems leave me to get well,
Now I wait an appointment, with a neurologist as well,
Wow, if it wasn't for the health business, I sure wouldn't get well.

Medical problems of my life, a life given by God,
Suffering to enrich me, to make me see the good in God,
God is my rock, suffering is my downfall,
But each time I think, God is with me as well.

Mary Jo West

THE NOT SO MERRY WIDOW

I rushed around the house for hours with duster and with vac
I vowed that not a vestige of attention would it lack
I washed my smalls and ironed my sheets, a busy bee was I
And wished my loyal spouse on hand to bring them in when dry
Well, then I found some tiles were loose, and sought a tube of gum
Hoping that thereby I need not have the builder come
But then I inadvertently slipped backward off a stool
And split my head wide open, so incompetent a fool.

My neighbours rallied round me, to the hospital I went
I've always thought these places were less than heaven sent
We waited and we waited, and we waited yet some more
I think we were regarded as the undeserving poor
No fairy came to rescue us by granting us a wish
I think the gnomes and goblins heaped contempt on us poor fish
Concern was for my neighbour, *I* had brought it on myself
This happening made mincemeat of our glorious National Elf.

And when, though all was done for me, they didn't have the staff
It's all these private hospitals that warrant the last laugh
We left the nurse, the doctor, and the trolley and the chair
The thought of not so wealthy people filled me with despair
For sitting on the rows of chairs, so woebegone their look
Three score of hopeful patients, having done things by the book
While I was home and comfy with perhaps a cup of tea
They still could sit for hours as they couldn't pay a fee.

Good old Aneurin must be turning in his grave
For he'd thought of all the suffering and the lives that he could save.

Doris Holland

FRAGILE

Seventeen young and naive,
I walked onto Ward 11,
As a Health Care Assistant I did not conceive,
How far we seemed from Heaven.

As I looked around at each patient in bed,
I'd see pain written in the lines of each face,
Many so ill they needed to be fed,
A challenge I fulfilled with God's grace.

In a side room a man lies waiting to die,
As disease eats up his bones,
I sit and hold his hand, mindfully asking God 'Why?'
This tragedy has occurred and why his family never phones.

Cardiac Arrest and the 'crash' team arrive,
We all have an important role to play no matter how small,
In vain a patient fails to revive,
And I faint at the shock of it all.

But amidst death, family turmoils and tears,
There would be days of much laughter,
With God's help to calm people's fears,
I thanked Him for the people He gave to me to look after.

Dawn Braidwood

W-HEALTH

National Health, called for in trust,
upon us all in hardness thrust.

Against our plea, 'Have a care,'
at first a service for all to share.

Cash for health, means of wealth,
done deliberately, and with stealth.

Indirectly a form of tax, from this
pursuit they never lax.

Profits first, people last,
no end to greed, their die is cast.

First your money (if you can pay),
but if not . . . you've had your day.

Managers walking through wards at will,
bearing medical staff ill-will.

We'll end up at end of queue,
operations for many are few.

Finding space to fit a bed.
Better still if most are dead.

Bide the time till next election,
your return, cause for objection.

'Eye-Write'

PATIENT PATIENT

'Be a patient patient,' to my impatient spouse I say,
As yet another courteous nurse says, 'please walk this way'.
This year has been a never ending nightmare,
While my husband's being treated with tender care.
Many hours we have spent twiddling our thumbs,
Ages sitting on chairs, result being numb bums.
The infection with which he has been plagued lingers on,
Now with each appointment his patience has finally gone.
'Be a patient patient,' I repeat once again,
Knowing each minute waiting is a terrible strain.
We look forward to the future, when my husband's well,
But when that is likely to be, nobody can tell.

Susan Mullinger

HELP

If you are unlucky enough to go to hospital
Trusting the doctors to make you well
I am sure it is not as bad as folk say
When needing tests or having an X-ray
The doctors are concerned to make folk well
It is not their wish to see folk ill
I am sure they all are doing their best
However, folk will complain and the rest
It is a great pity things have changed
And the NHS is de-arranged
With wards that have closed and empty beds
Can government ministers get it into their heads
That money is needed quick and fast
If the NHS is going to last
Waiting lists are unreasonably long
Before you get there, you may be 'gone'
But when you arrive you are treated well
How long you will stay you cannot tell
As soon as possible you are routed out
Sent home too soon without a doubt
Let us hold on fast to our NHS
Before it ends in a right old mess
It is not funny when you are not well
Ending up in hospital
The nurses work hard, long their day
It is time something is done to improve their pay
It is shameful having to make a guess
As to whether we will lose our NHS.

Evelyn A Evans

WHY I WAS MADE REDUNDANT

I used to work for the NHS
Until the government closed us down,
and sent the patients out into the world.
Then life became hard, I found.

I worked for them for nearly eight years.
Not a day off sick did I take.
Then the government sold the land,
and money in, they did rake.

I still think the NHS is good,
and the government treats them wrong.
Bit by bit it's going now.
The NHS won't last long.

Maria Arnott

A FREE HAIR-DO

I was admitted to the hospital,
for an op, on my left ear,
But after shaving off my hair, they changed their mind,
after I'd waited, for a year.

It was the day of my 60th birthday,
and I'd cancelled my party, to get the op,
But when I was handed, a hearing aid, instead,
it really made me hop.

I had to wear a head square, for some months,
as my hair was such a mess,
But the Health Board said, 'the surgeon wasn't to blame,'
'Cos the op, was never a success.

Jean Hendrie

THE NHS

Bureaucracy has brought a fall
        and lost the sight of where,
Priorities should lie with all
        hard pressed to gain health fair.

Doctors cannot give of their best
        as paperwork piles high,
The patients shunted without rest
        whilst harassed staff pass by.

The chief executive exhorts
        the cut in treatment cost,
And the losers from the reports
        are patients with cures lost.

Bureaucrats could not give a hoot
        with thoughts of money base,
Whilst patients die with ills acute
        through lack of treatment place.

Conveyor belt health practised wide
        to try to make ends meet,
But all is such a rush in tide
        you wear out hands and feet.

All have become items in play
        that dance to newest rule,
And government has not the way
        nor sense to change the fuel.

Finance is worshipped as the god
        by the Service bosses,
And patients are dismissed to sod
        when all count their losses.

Aileen Hopkins

MUMMY I KNOW YOU'RE THERE

Mummy I trust that you're there,
Though they had to ventilate,
I know you'll always be there but I think you'll have to wait.

Mummy I hear that you're there,
Through these panes of glass,
And when you whisper to me the time just seems to pass.

Mummy I feel that you're there,
Though I'm covered with tubes and wire,
The lightest touch from you lifts my spirit higher.

Mummy I guess that you're there,
Though while it is so bright,
I'm laid with goggles on to protect from therapy light.

Mummy I realise you're there,
You're the highlight of my day,
Before doctor's round, cares from my nurse and the lady from X-ray.

Mummy I smell that you're there,
Whenever you're in the room,
Your wonderful fresh washed skin and your subtle milky perfume.

Mummy I see that you're there,
I recognise your form,
When you sit close by to me I'll weather any storm.

Mummy I sense that you're there,
But until I manage to grow,
I'm kept warm in incubator, for how long I do not know.

Mummy I know that you're there,
For whichever way I lie,
I catch a glimpse of you whenever I open my eye.

'Mummy I'll always be here'

Rianne Cannon

A PATIENT OF THE NHS

I've had my share of hospitals
Have always had great care
The nurses were fantastic
The doctors had such flair
A patient of the NHS
I didn't have to pay
The service was impeccable
Kindness in every way
I couldn't speak more highly
Of the standard nursing care
And the daily food they served
You couldn't better anywhere
I guess I want to praise
The treatment of the NHS
On coming home much better
That's more than proof I guess

Jeanette Gaffney

WHAT'S HAPPENING TO OUR NHS?

The NHS is going down the drain,
when will the better times come back again.
Patients waiting on trolleys for hours and hours,
who should be tucked up in bed where you can take them flowers.
But it will be all right if you go private and lots of money you spend,
Although it worries us poor folk our National Health will have to end.

Maureen Kimpriktzis

HOSPITALS

The smell of antiseptic as one enters the door,
The clean and starchy aprons,
the shine upon the floor.
Doctors working long hours
as lives they strive to save,
Nursing staff and sisters,
The patients, being brave.

The skilful operations curing the sick and ill,
The path lab and the X-ray,
The penicillin pill.
The long day starting early,
Without much time for rest,
Fighting pain and fever
Giving nothing but their best.

Always very busy those who work in Casualty,
Ready, there and willing for each emergency.

This team that works together
with such great dedication,
How can we ever thank them
or show our appreciation.
We cannot repay their kindness
or the care they gladly give,
They tend us when we need them
and give the will to live.

Joan Heybourn

IN GRATITUDE I WRITE THIS

It's much maligned and criticised
In keeping with the modern trend
But our National Health is there for us
And on its staff we can depend
Whose doctors and the nurses
Whose dedication is plain to see
Are there to diagnose and cure
The ills of you and me

Frightened of the unknown
Lying in an unfamiliar bed
The pre-med pill, the soothing words
This is the moment that I dread
The sun shining through the window
Woke me up the following morn
Yes I had survived the surgeon's knife
It's as though I've been reborn

So in gratitude I write this
To those doctors and nurses all
Who staff each of our hospitals
And are there if we should call
Winter summer, night and day
Constantly under stress
We should offer our heartfelt thanks
For those who work for the NHS

Don Woods

THE NURSE'S DILEMMA

Nursing's a caring profession,
Needing stamina, compassion and skill
In dealing with patients' problems
With gentleness and goodwill.

In the modern climate of caring,
Much rests on ability to pay,
By surgeries, trusts and authorities;
Patients' welfare is left by the way.

The nurse tries so hard to tend the sick
In wards understaffed, supplies lacking;
Constantly rushing, to work to a plan
Shaped by non-medical backing.

She strives to fulfil her commitments,
Hampered by cuts over all;
No longer the job satisfaction,
Her standards have taken a fall.

Long gone is the personal rapport;
The bond between patient and nurse
Is severed by modern technology,
Dictated by rules of the purse.

She knows the fear of the patient
Is pleading for soothing words
Of comfort and reassurance,
But no time for her voice to be heard.

Little time for the dying patient
Needing someone to just hold his hand,
As he drifts in and out of existence,
En route for his promised land.

So much can be done by the personal touch
In easing the suffering and pain
Of a frightened human being,
Distressed in his anguished domain.

But nurses are now disillusioned,
Guilty, economically fettered;
No time for care and counselling
In a system they *know* could be bettered.

Ann Price

CARDIAC CRISIS

The blue light flashed down the hillside, ever nearer.
No sound yet.
Just as well - no need to add to the panic.
The noise of breathing engulfed the whole room,
Like blowing bubbles through a bowl of soup.
Her chest moved erratically in waves.
The muscle moving with all its might,
Fighting against a pressure equivalent to
The weight of a hundred breeze blocks.
A silent prayer.
Please hurry there can't be much strength left.
At last two tones heralded the arrival of,
Two efficient figures calmly disturbing the dawn.
Their uniforms matched the colour of her lips.
Swift action with nimble fingers flicked machinery.
Then her frail form was lifted into the waiting vehicle.
May she be delivered from danger by the power of drugs.

Anne Savan

BLUE GENES

Waiting in the corridor
Tense and staring at the floor
Endless coffee endless tea,
Afraid of new technology
Nurse approaches doctor waits
Waiting now to hear my fate
Embarrassment cold instrument
Trying not to hypervent
All over now time to relax
Arrange my blouse
Zip up my slacks
Feeling somewhat sore and tender
But just can't wait to
Change my gender!

Steph Needham

THE NHS EXPERIENCE (A TRUE STORY)

The NHS has saved my life!
Yet I knew nothing of it!
I only know that I collapsed
One day and nearly had it!

What really happened I don't know,
But it hadn't really oughter!
It seems I burst an aneurysm
Within my aorta!

The medics, surgeons, nurses too,
All did their skilful share
In mending me and giving me
Ten days intensive care!

I had no worry and no pain,
In comfort was I rested,
And yet it seems that many folk
Were really interested!

For, all unbeknownst to me,
The surgeons felt it drastic
And fitted up inside my chest
A new aorta - plastic!

So now, though not mechanical,
Nor really yet a robot,
I can with pride feel deep inside
Something that you ain't got!

Reg Hunter

GILES' TRIP TO THE DENTIST

Giles went to see the dentist today
As he needed an appointment straight away
They opened his mouth and looked at his teeth
His wisdom tooth gave him such terrible grief.

Laying back in the chair, his mouth open wide
Frightened to be there, he wanted to hide
The lights went on as these big eyes looked down
Giles sweated madly for he wanted to drown

The drill started up as he cried out in pain:
'I'm not coming back to this dentist again'
His tooth felt a pull as he jumped out his seat
Punched the poor dentist, knocked him right off his feet.

With blood pouring out and a bib round his throat
He spat on the pavement and started to choke
For he'd swallowed his tooth and his mouth was so sore,
So he never went back to the dentist no more.

So now he can't eat or light up a fag
This tale has turned out to be something quite sad
But if he's a good boy and does as requested
Then he might just be lucky and it won't get infected.

Louise Sullivan

THE FIRST CUT IS THE DEEPEST

This verse is ode to theatre blues
Baggy trousers soggy shoes
Complete the look with a paper hat
Not to worry if you look a p . . . !

Don your rubber gloves and mask
the stage is set for you the cast
Gas man begin with a brilliant induction
Lights! Music! Rev up the suction

There's a kind of hush the tensions rising
Soon the star will be arriving.
He's here *hail!* Sir Galahad
Othello Heathcliffe, the thief of Baghdad.

Crash of thunder *flash* of light
Splash of water and a thorough wipe.
Tie his gown mop his brow,
Meekly repose with a curtsy or bow.

Stand on your mark don't utter a sound
Soon you'll be lucky if your feet touch the ground.
Running here tripping there
Sparks are flying everywhere.

Poised he stands knife in hand
Surrounded by his merry band.
He makes the first cut the blood starts to pour
He's splashed the light the scrub nurse the floor.

'Don't panic!' he cries, 'we have the technology
I've studied for years and I have an ology!'
Crazed and frenzied he tackles the flow
Conquers the bleeder then basks in the glow

Is the first cut always the deepest?
The wound will be dressed in whatever is cheapest!

Angela Molloy

ARE YOU ASLEEP?

Are you asleep this little voice cries,
As I dream away, with very closed eyes.
Are you asleep, I have your pills,
To ease your aches and drive away your ills.
Oh why don't you leave me to sleep and hide,
Away from the tests, that wrecked my pride.
Tubes stuck here and there to wash out my inside,
Oh what an embarrassment, where can I hide?
And now to add insult and injury besides,
You wake me up from where I hide
Just to say, with a smile and a grin,
Here's your sleeping pill, have you had a good day,
And I hope you sleep well, you're here to stay.
Until tomorrow, it brings a new day.
What will happen, I do not know
But one thing's for sure, please tell me why
My sleeping pill comes, after I've closed my eyes?
And I'm dreaming away, a voice I hear cry
Are you asleep, I've a pill for you.
To help you sleep and dream to tomorrow anew.

Jill Munday

WELCOME

Oh! My goodness, my water has gone,
Off to hospital, won't take long,
Reached the hospital, then whisked away,
To a room, left on a bed to lay,
Waited a while, then examined too,
This is the moment, my baby is due,
The nurse took my temperature, blood pressure OK,
Into the delivery room, I'm on my way,
One pain, two pain, three pain and four,
These contractions are getting more and more,
Here we are, all prepared,
A girl or boy, I don't care,
Another pain, give me some air,
Puffing and panting, I can see some hair,
This is it, the baby's to come,
I need more air, give me some,
Take it steady, blow blow blow,
Here it is, the head does show,
Then a breath, for one more time,
Everything here is going fine,
I hear a cry, my bundle of joy,
Well my dear, you have a boy,
Oh! This feeling of delight,
My son in my arms, this wonderful sight,
The nurses doctors all who were there,
Gave me every moment of care,
They were there, all the time for me,
Without their help where would I be,
It was all done on the NHS,
I just rate them being the very best.

Lynn Hallifax

THE KNIVES ARE OUT!

Like a hundred, thousand others,
I climbed into my bed,
thinking of the coming day
with a sense of doom, of dread.
What was ahead, I dare not think,
I would take things as they came,
and come they did, so very fast -
no two nurses were the same.
They came with jabbing needles,
and other torturous things -
it made not the slightest difference
be we commoners or kings!
Then came the day we'd awaited
with feelings of great fear,
the surgeons were all ready,
the knives were drawing near!
In regal state, in virgin white,
wheeled in, one by one,
to have this out, or that repaired,
we didn't know, 'til it was done.
Awaking to the same old ward,
and nurses smiling faces,
of being sick, and aching
in the most *peculiar* places!
The time then passed so quickly
it was all in a haze,
but of the hospital and staff
I have nought but the highest praise.

Joyce Hockley

NATIONAL HEALTH SERVICE

I worked as an orderly for twenty-one years
Helped to care for elderly people
Some had such sad tales to tell
It reduced me near to tears

My days were very busy
With little time to stop
Tea breaks and lunch I often missed
So I could cover all my jobs

I have many happy memories
Of my days working on the wards
And of the lovely old folks
Their smile was my reward

Gillian Morrisey

NIGHT DUTY, ST THOMAS' HOSPITAL WINTER 1958

The dark ward at night.
The nurse, under the light,
The white-capped centre of a web whose strands
Stretch left to the dim-bulbed entrance, and right
To the balcony door.
Slow-flowing, the river winds
Through Westminster. Big Ben strikes four;
Now is the time for dying -
But no-one dies tonight.

This is no place of rest.
The patients fidget, like fledglings in a nest
Foiled in flying;
They rustle and cough, moan and sigh.
She takes the torch and makes her way
Past the sick sleepers. 'Nurse' cries one -
Two eyes caught in the beam
Plead for a basic need; the nurse
Hurries to the icy sluice
For the clattering pan,
Hands fumbling numb.
She swills a sheet and hangs it on the balcony
To stiffen with excrement and frost.

Here's no romance, adventure, drama to excite;
Only the hourly vigil to repeat.
Personal feelings, dreams, and aims are lost
When slow and weary feet
Tread creaking boards on monotonous patrol;
Responding to the call of nature, and the call
For sleep, and the cry of pain, and the tears of weakness, all
Through the endless, cold and lonely night.

Margaret Sparshott

TO 'LIL'

'Twas on a day in hot July, my call came for to go,
To Wellingboro' Cottage Hospital, not one soul did I know,
With the first performance over, the jabs in arm, the pokes in tum,
Me thought I'd take a walk outside, and to a ward did come,
Peering through the windows wide, I saw three ladies there,
A Mrs Toup, a Mrs Tite, and a Pole with straightish hair,
Now Mrs Toup she talked a lot, but 'twas music to the ear,
Although the subject often was my poor old tum I fear,
Mrs Tite a widow was and she from Rothwell came,
And fate decreed that she and I would one day meet again,
Goodbye to buttons, bottles, clips, the time came for to roam,
'Twas then we found we shared a room at convalescent home,
Now Lil, she was a generous soul, not as her name implied,
She'd often sing and tell such yarns we laughed until we cried,
And oh the fun and games there were in bedroom number eleven,
They said the peals of laughter could be heard in number seven,
The very Irish 'divvil' lurked in Kitty Darby's eyes,
Especially when in someone's bed she'd popped a big surprise,
There was gracious, quiet Carmen, who came from Trinidad,
Gay West Indian Norah, such a sunny nature had,
Poor Pam Jones from Rushden, on the outing caught a chill,
Spent three whole days confined to kip, on account of being ill,
And if for any reason downstairs you should go,
You'd find us sitting knitting on the veranda in a row,
Now Lil a rug was making and the bacca fumes rose high,
And there I'd sit amongst them, getting kippered high and dry,
I'm back in Corby now, the gang are scattered wide,
And only letters link the friends I found inside
It took an operation and convalescence too
To bring together *Ann* and *Lil*, *Good luck* my dear and God bless you.

Ann Moiser

THE ONE THAT GOT AWAY

(A tribute to a brilliant surgeon, Mr Firth)

'Don't worry, you'll be all right' he said,
Just to instill hope in my worried head,
'We'll operate after we've done a scan'.
Such faith I had in this clever man

I look back now after twenty healthy years,
And think of my sadness and night-time tears,
How I prayed for some help to quell my fear,
It's cancer they whispered 'Oh the poor dear'.

Into His hands I gave myself
To work through this surgeon to restore my health
Now I say to others 'Trust and pray
It happened to me, the one that got away'.

Yona Geddes

MY SECOND 'OP' AT MORRISTON HOSPITAL 1985

Two years ago I had a 'run'
in the other hospital, Singleton.
I had the 'op' that proved OK
Many thanks to 'them' I say
For getting me fit and well,
Now another tale I will tell.
This time when illness got me down
It was to Morriston (yes, with *gown*).
To put me right, they do intend
I'm sure they will make me mend
So quite content, I find myself, John
in the hands of a super 'throng'
These simple words may be crude
But to express my thanks it is 'good'
So to all Morriston, I say
You all deserve a bigger pay
Thanks to all for being so kind
I must stop, and let thoughts unwind.

John C Jarratt

NO HOPE SERVICE (A GERIATRIC LAMENT)

Past the 'sell-by' date?
Begrudged 'room on the shelf'?
Then get a second opinion
After all - it's *you* - *your own self*

Consultants leave the old 'uns high and dry
Dole out the Valium with a smile and a lie
Euthanasia's a blessing
They (privately) cry

More work for the gravediggers
More smoke to the pyres
Queue for the golden gates
Or descend to the fires

Too old at 40?
More than 40 to go?
The little white pills
Lure with a radiant glow

Suicide's dirty? Not on your life
First make sure there's enough for the wife
Mustn't be selfish, both must rejoice
Toast each other with joy
You've made the right choice!

Bryn Bartlett

THE WAITING ROOM

NHS patients line the walls of the bright, sunny waiting room.
There's an anxious old lady sitting in a wheelchair, face filled with gloom.
A tired young mum, heavily pregnant with number two.
A chatty lady full of ailments, but still taking an optimistic view.
Elderly men reading magazines, finding them of great interest.
A tanned lad from a building site, wearing a dusty vest.
A man waiting for his elderly aunt, faces the wall with a blank look.
And a woman writes something unintelligible in a green book.
The receptionists constantly tap at their keyboards,
Trying to sort out appointments for the chaotic hordes.
But eventually, they all go into the doctors and are seen.
It's been a long wait, but the people were friendly and the room clean.
We moan about the Health Service, but it seems to do its erratic best.
It's still an important factor in what makes this country a cut above the rest.

Linda Miller

THE NHS

I was a nurse
In the NHS
Studied and learned
passed my exams
            In the NHS.
Beds and bedpans
Injections and enemas
Medicine and comfort
I gave to all
            In the NHS.
The work was hard
But I loved it so
Babies to cuddle
And children small
            In the NHS.
I loved them all
As they strove to get well
Lots did but others were brave
            In the NHS.
I prayed with the dying
And sought to ease their fears
'God is good' I said
And so was
            The NHS.

Olive Crombie

SOUTHMEAD HOSPITAL BRISTOL
K WARD (INFECTIOUS DISEASES)

There's a little ward at Southmead, that seems kept out the way,
For although it's known as K Ward, it's marked with a small 'k',
Ten beds in isolation, each in its own room,
Each patient there infected, with an ill that could spell doom,
Salmonella, plague, and cholera, TB, AIDS, and mumps,
And terrible diseases, with suppurating lumps,
Poison that's turned septic, diphtheria and flu,
Anything infectious, is all transferred hereto,
So just who are these nurses, who staff this dreadful ward,
Looking after people, who are almost under guard,
Nurses are all angels, whether cream, brown, black or white,
I know I could not handle, some of these ghastly sights,
But in this little 'k' ward, with the dread diseases listed,
You'll meet a kind of angel, you never thought existed,
Patients in extremis, you wouldn't care to touch,
Are tended with devotion, these days you don't see much,
I don't remember reading any write-up of these girls,
Who after all are special, like you find a special pearl,
They do their work in secret, in this ward kept out the way,
I don't expect they're given, any special rate of pay,
But should you have to visit, some poor soul in here,
And see the things they have to touch, and mess they have to clear,
I think that some reporter, their banner should unfurl,
And tell the Bristol people, about some very special girls.

Charles H Boyett

CHANGED DAYS

I have worked in the NHS,
For twenty years or more,
Many changes I have seen,
I don't know what's in store,
Cut-backs just in everything,
Saving money too,
Seems their only pastime,
In this service meant for you,
We have changed to Trust now,.
and money's always tight,
I don't know if we'll make it,
What a sorry sight,
The day they privatised it,
Was a grave mistake I fear,
I only hope it works out well,
Sometimes I shed a tear,
For people who are in, then out,
Before they're ready to,
Two days later they come back,
Re-admitted, this is true,
Before they're ready to go home,
They're sent home anyway,
Without the back-up, they deserve,
What's things coming to, today,
Life is precious to us all,
We're vulnerable when sick,
So I just pray it comes out well,
And the NHS will click,
For many people need health care,
Looked after tenderly,
I hope the caring does not cease,
That would be sad, to see.

Janette Campbell

WISDOM TEETH

I was in pain my mouth was swollen.
'I'm afraid they will have to come out,'
My dentist compassionately said.
The next thing I knew, there I was
Lying in a hospital bed.
Down to the theatre I did go
With thoughts of never returning!
The anaesthetist was marvellous, so discerning,
When I awoke back up on the ward
I felt I had been cut up with a sword,
One look in the mirror gave me a fright
I had turned into a hamster overnight!
My cheeks were so swollen, my mouth was so sore,
They took out not one, but four.
Time to go home now, just after one day
But I felt so ill, I wanted to stay.
'We have patients waiting for your bed,'
The ward sister abruptly said,
I burst into tears, I was in a state
And all that I wanted was for my mouth to deflate!
One of the nurses was so very caring
Popping in and out to see how I was faring,
But the bed they did want, so it was time to go home,
I felt left outside, just like a garden gnome!
I can't blame the staff, as they were all very kind,
'It's the management,' they said,
So I vacated my bed.
When I returned home, I became very ill
An infection set in, I was given some pills,
Three courses of antibiotics, painkillers as well,
I felt it was a living hell.
But now it's all over and I'm back on my feet,
I never want to be reminded
Of my wisdom teeth.

Stephanie S Hall

THE OTHER SIDE OF THE COIN

Being a nurse for twenty odd years
Loving my work, take away patients' fears
I believe today their title is client
If only the system were still as reliant

To get to the point I ended up in an asylum
Quite a shock to my equilibrium
A point in my years, can't cope with life
The usual story, husband wife

Took to the bottle, take away reality
More than once, near fatality
The road to hell, blow upon blow
The loss of worth only a drinker will know

The hospital certainly saved my life
Only a drunk knows the strife
The guilt the shame of losing your sanity
Stress you cause, leaves no vanity

Strange to awaken to hospital smells
Talks routine the ringing of bells
I'd prayed for years, please make me well
To think what I'd done, my eyes swell

The power in that bottle, thank God I see
All too clearly how it affected me
Only with help from people who cared
The precious ones, the ones who shared

Today I'm alive, oh so aware
What price sanity, to those over there
A thin fine line once you cross over
You can never go back, if you want to recover

The things in your life so precious so dear
A day at a time there is no fear
Put back into life, contribute with faith
Making amends, perhaps some grace . . .

Jean Tennent Mitchell

DOCTOR KNOWS BEST

They did not listen they did not know
Pain is present now but in time it will go
Take this pill dear girl relax go to bed
It is not such a problem perhaps all in your head
But doctor, doctor, there is a problem I'm sure
Can't you see that my tummy is swollen and sore
Don't worry, don't worry, just try to forget
A result of adhesions a blockage I expect
But can't you do something this has happened before
I will prescribe you some pills take two, three, or more.

Colin Taylor

MEDICALLY SPEAKING
IT'S A SOBERING THOUGHT

I took 'several aspirin'
but, still 'it persists'
'The world spins around . . . '
even though . . . 'I'm not p . . . . . !'

Barry Howard

OUR MATRONS

Sick people don't need managers,
With economic gifts,
But qualified good nurses,
Who care for them in shifts.
When they took away our matrons,
And axed all discipline,
The patients were the losers,
A major public sin.
Today you find in hospitals
There aren't any rules,
With balance sheet decisions,
The place is run by fools.
The visitors can stay all day
With television loud,
The wards are unisex to please
The social worker crowd.
And in the streets you'll see also
Ward uniforms galore,
Picking up bacteria
And viruses by the score.
Who'd let a nurse with unkempt hair,
Hang over open sore,
With scarlet nails and earrings,
We would be shown the door.
But I remember when the wards
Were sanctuaries of peace,
Clean calm and order, crisp white sheets
True nursing did not cease.
So what we need are matrons back,
Who daily did a round,
Devoted to the patients' needs
Not to the powerful pound.

Mary Lefebvre

CAROLINE

She has a name few people know,
She roams the streets, nowhere to go.
They closed down her home, shut the gate.
The ministers in power have sealed her fate.

For years looked after day and night,
Sometimes she smiled, sometimes she'd fight.
Mental illness sad but true
Could happen to anyone, but what can we do.

In the infinite wisdom of the powers that be
They are shutting the doors of this old sanctuary,
Where mental illness was treated with care,
Help from nurses and doctors always there.

Where this young lady lived, secure safe and warm.
Now out on her own she must face the storm.
No-one to turn to when frightened and lost,
So sad she must suffer for those who cut costs.

One day the errors may be seen,
But for the years that lie between
For Caroline no peace, no fun,
To her the damage has been done.

Valerie Green

TO CARE FOR OTHERS

I have to get up at five thirty to be at the station for six,
So I get to the ward on time for my shift, to care for all those who are sick.
There is breakfast, then 'obs', then washes and baths, then dressings to name but a few,
Of the things that we do every day of the week for each person coming in new.
We do doctors rounds and go to X-ray, then take or collect from theatre,
And hope that the ones who feel dreadfully sick will soon start to feel so much better.
When at the end of a really long shift we wearily make our way home,
We know that tomorrow we'll be back again, to care for all the new ones who come.

Winifred Jenkins

JUST A THOUGHT

The district nurse came to see me
She made me feel so pleased
It's surprising how her kindness
Soon put me at my ease

She spoke kind words of wisdom
As she put my dressing on
And she made sure before she went
That nothing had gone wrong

She helps me with my doctor
And dressings for myself
Since she has been calling
I find improvement in my health

I would like to thank her for her kindness
For what she has done for me
To think that all this kindness
I get it all for free.

Bert Booley

OUR PROMISE TO YOU

O ur dedicated nurses
U nderstand the fears you share
R elated to your illness; so

P lease let us show we care.
R eassurance may be given
O r we'll talk each problem through,
M ake us share your burdens
I f you feel they're troubling you.
S taff are here to teach you
E verything you need to know,

T o understand the treatment
O r the steps you should follow.

Y ou'll learn within our guidance
O vercoming all your fears, that
U pheaval of dialysis is not as bad as it appears.

Sarah Maycock

NEONATAL NURSE

A neonatal nurse
Is somebody who cares
for special little babies
whether one or three or pairs

Some are very small
and may need some ventilation
We give them lots of care
and never leave our station

Lots of different babies
some not so very small
need our looking after
and the docs on call

These babies need our love
and their families as well
to mum and dad especially
everything we tell

Needles, drips and monitors
are all part of our work
to make our babies better
there's no job that we shirk

The unit's very hot
and we often feel like cursing
but there's really nothing like
neonatal nursing.

Lyn Collins

LIFE BEFORE THE NHS!

Wartime - and the sirens wail,
Ambulances arriving without fail!

But uniforms always spic and span,
Starched collars and cuffs - and a 'no jewellery' ban.

Bed-pans, trolleys - put out of sight
Before the ward sister comes for the night!

Medical students trailing round the ward,
Gaining knowledge - their only reward;
People coming in for one shilling and three,
So they could practise their anatomy!

Harley Street surgeons giving their time,
And not even charging anyone a dime!

Doctors lecturing till one,
And, hopefully, then there was time for fun!

Rationing - very little cheese or meat,
So have to be grateful for what you *can* eat!

No complaints from patients or staff -
'There's a war on!' So let's have a laugh.

'The next bomb may have your name on it,
So keep on smiling and keep fit!'

Good old days, with no new techniques,
But kindness and love from the heart always speaks.

A gentle touch and a calming hand,
Brought health and life back through a small, brave band!

Betty Wilson

NEWTOWN NURSES

God bless our nurses one and all
For answering their chosen call
Without them though, we must confess
We'd see NHS in an even bigger mess
Patients are tended with loving care
No better service anywhere
Passing the men's ward there one day
I heard the sister loudly say -
No . . . you can't take the Night Nurse twice a day
Everything else on the menu's free
But 'naughties' aren't allowed by me
Proof they'd nursed him back to health
Now he can't behave himself

A patient over Christmas said
I'm not sorry I'm here in bed
I'd have missed all this you see
Nobody lives in my flat but me
Christmas Eve the Silver Band
played in the ward and it was grand
Next, carol singers came in sight
They sang to us of 'Holy Night'
So . . . nurses not to be outdone
Performed a panto, that was fun

The Christmas Fayre, the lady stated
Was next to none, plus three-star rated
Presents, trimmings, and a tree
Look around and you can see
The nurses are so kind to you
Even take us by armchair to the loo
Which proves we have a life of leisure
'Cos even the Queen don't get that pleasure
Reminiscing that night, I wrote these verses
And raised my glass to the Newtown nurses

Bell Ferris

FIRST RATE NATIONAL HEALTH BUNCH

A very normal day it was as we completed chores.
Then husband went to have a rest as oft he'd done before.
Suddenly he gave a cry as if in dreadful pain.
As I hurried to him I heard him call my name.
I looked, then picked the phone up, 'Please doctor come at once,'
She did and having seen him, sent for an ambulance.
The men with that were top class, they really were supreme,
Handling him so gently, careful and serene.
At Addenbrookes the doctors diagnosed heart attack.
Working hard to help him as I quietly sat back.
In intensive care ward a sister by his side,
Keeping close watch on him, helping my fears subside.
Suddenly she pressed a bell, at same time said to me,
'Will you go outside and wait, this is emergency'.
As I got outside door saw doctor run with speed,
Down corridor, into ward to help sister succeed
In job of saving man's life, but when thanks I gave,
Said, 'That's what we're here for, to nurse folk and them save'.
Each day he was kept there it always was the same.
Treated him so kindly, even used his first name.
Let me sit beside him from early morn till night,
Never heard them grumble at any task in sight.
This was National Health work, which if we'd had to pay,
Could not have been bettered, in any single way.
Nurses very cheerful as they rubbed along,
Doctors very helpful, explaining what was wrong.
Cheery little wardmaids smiling did their work,
In the time he spent there we saw *no-one* shirk.
That hospital was tip-top in saving my man's life,
First rate National Health bunch, says a very grateful wife.

Barbara Goode

MRS A HARTLEY SEEKETH THE TRUTH

Dear Spirit Angels thank you for guiding me
to Mrs Hartley, the said lawyer above
Whom I met and shook hands firmly with
To discuss an operation I had which went sadly wrong.

Now with her knowledge of our medical law
I had to have faith and trust with all that I saw
My medical records she requested for me
to lay down on her desk
For her to read and analyse when she felt best
Now with this task I have entrusted and
laid before thee.
Please, I implore, seeketh the truth and bring to the fore
Mistakes can happen, of this we are aware
But with your assessment of my records we must attain
Somebody must account for the pain and suffering
I have endured and sustained
Dear Spirit Angels, please help and guide
Mrs Hartley to plant a seed of truth and light
That I was right and no human being
Should have to endure this awful plight.

Joyce Brown

LET THERE BE LIGHT!

The dull pain in my lower back gradually got worse.
I took warm baths, headache pills, as the pain I began to curse!
It was only six am and I had no alternative choice,
'Can you send the doctor please?' I whispered in guilty voice.
He diagnosed *'Lumbago*! Making your daughter's wedding dress has
taken its toll of your vertebrae, they're under extreme stress.'
Lumbago it was not! Neither was it option two, as an alternative diagnosis,
'It might be a kidney stone. Have you been to the loo?'
Within an hour I was in St Luke's! My neck was totally numb!
They gave me a lumbar puncture *ooh!* And another in my bum!
By now I was in some far-off place. Oblivious to the frenzy and pace
As an international team worked non-stop behind the screen.
Demented family and friends phoned around the clock for news.
Mum said 'Well, I never! Meningitis! But our Joyce is a fighter,
and this battle please God, don't let her lose!'
For days I lay there all gaunt and still with doctors attending
throughout the long nights,
My eyes were unable to focus, and despised the faintest of lights.
Flowers and cards adorned my little room so many tributes of love,
But the greatest gift as we all know is the one of life from above.
The swiftness of the illness made it all so clear, how fragile life is,
And oh so very dear!
My mother came and bathed me as she had bathed me as a child,
her eyes averting mine should I see the fear in her smile.
'You're in good hands here,' she sighed 'but why oh why is it you my love?'
As she gently dried my arms and legs her eyes automatically looked above.
But here I am to tell the tale, to be thankful. I pray each night and
smile at the moment I got well.
The Irish nurse with her deft little hands took the shades away and
yelled 'There you are my pretty lady, now let there be light!'
I wondered why God hadn't taken me. Was there some work on earth
to be done?
Yes.You see he needed my beloved little mum.

Joyce M Hefti-Whitney

DETERIORATION

Our Health Service was the best,
the greatest in the world.
Now it's falling far behind
and swords at it, are hurled.

Our doctors were a caring lot,
they made us feel so calm.
But now it's just injections,
like on a factory farm.

Our nurses used to hold us,
and soothe us with their powers.
Now, they stand around in groups,
and chat away for hours.

Woe to those who need an OP.
They wait around for years.
Racked by pain and trouble,
and filled with un-named fears.

Prescriptions handed out by day.
By night, they haunt our dreams.
No-one has time to talk to us,
or *that's* the way it seems.

Experiments on Animals
won't make *us* well at all.
It's just a great scientific con.
Our backs against the wall.

Our health will just deteriorate.
Harsh fantasies fill our heads.
While Government plays around with us
until we're all stone dead!

Daf Richards

IN HOSPITAL

I was in hospital for a short time
To have a little rest
They said I'd had a stroke
And needed a few tests.

I was in hospital for a short time
Boy the food was good
But when I asked for more
Somehow I was misunderstood.

I was in hospital for a short time
And was glad to get out
To get better at home they said
Where folks don't scream and shout.

Keith L Powell

NURSING 1941-1981

I was, still am, a nurse
To those in need of care,
Called by any name for those in need *she* is *nurse,*
In my time no day or night was ever the same
Except the courage, anguish and pain.

With time I was lonely, strangely apart,
Oh yes I had my children, love and laughter,
But all that pain does something to one's heart,
Trivialities were not for me,
Politicians filled me with anger,
They are still a pain.

Caring you see is an art,
Business and politicians just do not know
Caring for the anguished and dying they have no part,
They said to me, you give too much time,
They must learn you cannot always be there,
Their families now must give the care,
It broke so many hearts, including mine.

By the way, this they had to say to me,
Nurses must not expect much money,
They have such fulfilment, such satisfaction
Don't you see?
My reply . . .'To care one needs a heart and humility.'

Florence Andrews

MY NHS EXPERIENCE

Recently visiting a hospital,
for an important scan,
all the staff were most helpful
doing all they can.

Couples waiting patiently
for their certain turn.
So they know something today
to see what they can learn.

There is a little girl plucking
a string on a guitar toy,
She is playing happily,
filled with lots of joy.

Some children are prancing impatiently
parents are getting cross.
Hoping to change this appointment
where's that blinking boss?

This little girl is now
getting on my nerves.
Her mum and dad promise her sweeties,
this she does not deserve.

Yet there's a solemn gentleman,
sitting on my left.
He seems to be in a dream world,
his mind he just has left.

The couple now sitting opposite
start to quarrel and chat,
how they are going to decorate
their cosy little flat.

At last it is now my turn
To get my x-ray done.
Let me get home to peace and quiet
and sit quietly with my mum.

Mary Farr

AFTER THE CATARACT OPERATION

Slowly, but surely, she was losing her sight;
Reading and knitting, her favourite pastimes,
Were becoming impossible.
Time can be a cruel enemy to aged eyes
When a body can do little else but sit and dream
of times past;
And days to come the harder to bear
When simple ambitions, like finishing a book or sweater,
Remain unfulfilled.

She had her longed-for operation -
And the magical re-creation of sight
Gave her a new lease of life.
Two days of life-enhancement on the NHS,
Three years of book - and wool - devouring followed;
Until that wretched day when she awoke
To pain and blindness once again.

The skin had once more grown over one eye.
The NHS optician was quite blasé,
"We'll have to send you back again' he said,
'But it's not urgent' he added, unempathetically.
She thought 'I'm ninety one, I can do precious little
But read, and knit sweaters for orphans in Bosnia and India . . .
I want, I need to do these things.'

Her doctor, to whom she was referred, agreed with her -
Marked the envelope to the hospital *'Urgent.'*

And, as I write, she sleeps,
Hoping that the letter from the hospital arrives soon,
Inviting her once again to partake of her small portion of life -
Her age-old right to enjoy life in her nonagenarian,
And therefore limited, but nonetheless valid way -
Before it's too late.

J Margaret Service

NHS EXPERIENCE

I trained as a nurse in 1969
When the NHS were better times
I wore apron - starched stiff and white
A bronze buckle was polished bright.
I tended most geriatric cases
Saw many wrinkled, tired faces.
They were happier times of old
Interesting memories I was told.
There was more time to care
Elders always felt welcome there
Nurses then were much more keen
Worked well in a close-up team,
I also worked in *Isolation*
With many varied, interesting patients,
Mostly younger, stronger ones there
But still needing tender loving care.
Infections and diseases from so far away.
I was *gowned up* to keep germs at bay.
The days were busy with lots to do
A quick turnover of patients new.
I've been a patient too on the NHS
Needed an operation and time to rest,
It was strange being on the other side
But in pals I could confide.
I peeped at charts hanging on the bed
Knowing well what they said.
Nurses rush round more these days
More machines on which to gaze.
Less time for moments shared
Less time for tender, loving, care!

Sheila Waller

AT HOME

They say my room has such a lovely view;
It's my home now, or so the nurses say
But days pass by, with nothing much to do.

Four times a day they wheel me to the loo
Then pad me up: I'm ready for the day.
They say my room has such a lovely view.

My clothes are fixed with Velcro; my left shoe
Falls off. They sit me in my usual bay,
But days pass by, with nothing much to do.

They feed me some pills and puréed stew
Served always on the same Formica tray;
They say my room has such a lovely view.

Then once a week they bring out some shampoo
To wash my hair; they won't admit it's grey
But days pass by, with nothing much to do.

The home is purpose-built, the staff are new
And try to help. I do not want to stay.
They say my room has such a lovely view
But days pass by, with nothing much to do.

Philip Woodrow

NO HEALTH SERVICE

'Can I -'
Gone. Just like the first time.
It's like a foreign place in here. No-one speaks my language.
'Could you -'
Gone again. Like a juggernaut this time, barging through.
Like I'm invisible or something.
'Does anyone hear me?'
'My friend - '
A quick nod but her thoughts are elsewhere,
shuffling past me
like I am some sort of street pedlar.
So I stand back and watch.
This place is like all the others:
different accents, different cultures,
different people, different staff,
same attitude, same system, same ignorance.
Everyone alien to me, but looking for the same thing I am.
'I need help' says another in the corner,
the busy room too cramped and stuffy.
But he's also ignored. Just like me.
Funny feeling this,
but I'm not laughing.
Feeling like a production line product -
quick fit here, quick snap there . . . next!
But we're all last in the line.
Before or after that guy in the corner?
Who knows . . . nobody cares.
No Health Service.
We call it the NHS -
for short.

Andrew Jones

LOST KEY

Many years ago (the forties
No doubt before your time)
I became a *mental* nurse
And rules I had to sign.
To *never* strike a patient
Be calm and *always* kind,
But most important rule of all . . .
My *keys*, never left, for someone else to find.

This, in the early days of the NHS
Really put us to the test.
Supplies there were a-plenty,
Drugs and Penicillin flowed,
No worry of expenses,
Oh! How the prescriptions rose . . .
To suggest we were extravagant,
Well, that wouldn't be a lie . . .
. . . Mind you, we nurses took our lead
From others, way up high.

Now we are in the 90's
The NHS has not changed,
The waste is still around,
. . . But now it's grown in numbers
And seems quite out of bounds.

There are, of course, some changes
With patients now called 'Clients,'
And all doors are open free,
But sometimes, I do wonder . . .
. . . Just *who* has lost
the key?

Joyce Humphrey

A HEALTH VISITOR'S LAMENT - OR G P FEVER

Oh! I must go down to the surgery,
For the week, it has just begun,
And patients queue for the doctor, the loo
And some are there just for the fun.
And the phones ring,
And the kids yell,
And the doctor's waiting;
Computer's bust,
I'm coping - just . . .
But Miss Brown's there fainting.

Oh, I must go home from the surgery
Though the roads are covered with ice;
If I break my neck, then what the heck -
Just to get out of here will be nice.
My hair's going grey;
Roll on the day
When I will be retiring,
The door's locked,
The phone's stopped -
And I'm expiring!

Pat Moore

INTENSIVE CARE

Flick the switch
pull out the tubes.
Remove the life support.

Close her eyes
replace her teeth.
Tie ribbon around her feet.

Dress her in a paper shroud
wrap her in a sheet.
Now send her on her way.

Jane Burdall

COMMUNITY LIFE IN THE NHS

Community Services are reeling.
We are reaching the very ceiling
Of our staffing levels and expertise.
Very soon we'll be on our knees!

We'll be praying for a 'Revolution.'
Looking for the 'Final solution,'
To end our endless working day,
And frustrations of our take-home pay!

Time saved here, and time saved there,
When do we have time to care?
We are drowning in a sea of paper,
Computer returns, to compile data.

We may long for the days before 'Trust'
When the NHS was National, and just.
Now, we are told what to do,
Our autonomy lost! Who is who? . . .

We may feel despondent at grass root level,
But, our managers are in less peril.
They sit in comfort, in their seat,
Safe with power and no sense of retreat!

Onward, and upward is the way to go,
We shall survive, this we know.
Changes are challenges every day,
'Mission accomplished,' is what we say!

G E Harrison

ANGELS ONE FIVE?

'Was that you?'
I joked with the patient
As I lowered the creaking bed.
Thoughts of shift's end
Lurking in my shattered head.

'Ha! Ha! Ha!'
The well trained body cried.
I smiled almost electronically.
It was expected of me
The new generation; ironically.

'Oh! Nurse you are a wag!'
The statement was made.
To reinforce my saint-hood.
Another chip from
The block of the Good.

'Well, I try'
I replied quite honestly
Wiping the mirth from my eyes
Recharging my tears for
The next under-the-bed surprise.

Mark R Bonson

DESPERATE PRAYERS

It is the longest hour of night,
And mid-summer.
So he lies on the bed, naked; like fire.
His mind muddled on morphine.
Thoughts strangled.
She touches his face and witnesses his struggle;
Replaces the sheet that resembles a shroud,
Over bones that resemble a body.
It's too soon . . .
Not yet . . .
Tomorrow he will die.
But now, on the mantelpiece, the cards.
'Get well soon,' on every one.
Misplaced wishes.
Desperate prayers.

Jennifer Antell

THE LAST BREATH

I worked as an auxiliary in a hospital caring for the old
I would sit and chat to them and listen to stories they told
Some enjoyed the company having no family or friends
No-one to see them through until the very end.

I fed the very frail who were far too incapable
Victims of strokes or illnesses I would help them all
I would wash and bath them and make sure they were dry
Some were so embarrassed occasionally they'd cry.

The old lose their dignity it is an awful way to live
I was happy helping them I had so much to give
So one day when I am old, I hope I will get by
Without being dependable on someone I want to slip away and die.

I saw a man who did just that but it was still a shock
His breathing changed rapidly so I checked against a clock
And made him comfortable while I waited for him to die
It was a sad experience but amazingly I did not cry.

Deborah Butcher

BEING 'PATIENT'

I tried to lift the patient but he would not leave his seat.
The sister yelled -
'You wally, you're standing on his feet!'
I said, 'I'm really sorry,' and tried to make amends.

But as I stooped to get his slippers, I trod upon his lens.
'I truly am so sorry, I didn't see them there.
Is this your tie that's trapped beneath the chair?
Try to keep calm sir, I'll have it out in a sec!'

But as I bent to release the tie,
A finger caught him squarely in the neck!
'Please forgive me sir; you see, I'm fairly new round here.'

'Oh that's alright dear, I've had rough treatment before . . .
Now when was it . . .? Ah, I remember, it was as a *prisoner-of-war!*

Neville Hawkins

A HOSPITAL VISIT

When I saw my friend beside her hospital bed
she was busily tackling her steak and kidney pie.
It was so hard for me to realise the truth.
Just days ago she had been in intensive care
following a heart attack and breathing problems.

She had known constant supervision day and night.
Now here she was, back in an ordinary ward,
The side table resembling a florist's shop,
not to mention the attractive bowl of fruit.

Proudly she told me she had got forty six cards.
How lovely to know that so many people cared.
As I sat talking to her how my heart rejoiced.
She was so full of all that had happened to her
and the wonderful kindness of the hospital staff.

She even managed to have an occasional grumble
so I knew that she was truly on the mend!
Most of all though her sense of humour shone through.
I find that humour often triumphs over adversity.

Already too she was itching in her frustration
to get back home and carry on her ordered routine.
While I was there with her the physiotherapist came.
Shortly she was up and running on her zimmer frame.
What determination she showed despite the pain
Slowly out of her chair into an upright position.

Today she just managed to move a tiny distance.
Tomorrow she would go further. Tomorrow. Another day.
I left her tired out from sheer exertion
yet possessing a totally positive attitude.
No complaints! The NHS treated her like a queen
but you know just perhaps she was!

John Christopher Cole

FINANCIAL CAVITY

My NHS dentist
Charges eighty percent
Does he fill only four fifths
Or drill one fifth less depth?

My teeth are not aching
But this dentist assures me
I need seven new fillings
Pounds, one hundred and forty.

Marcus Pond

NO, I WASN'T MAD, JUST STRESSED . . .

N o, I wasn't mad, just stressed, it was the job.
E verybody said 'Pull yourself together, Elaine, you're a Police Officer'
. . . I so so
R eally wanted to - oh how I tried but the dark, dark
V eil seemed to close over me, like a rain cloud ready to burst.
O nce in hospital, I felt safe and secure, like an embryo in the womb . . .
no strait jackets, or padded cells, no men in white coats.
U niforms did not exist; nurses and doctors were known by first names
- and became my friends, my confidantes.
S leep was all I seemed to do, at the start - or cry - recharging your
batteries - I was told, nature's way.
B oth men and women from all walks of life were in the ward
- all with varying problems; we mixed freely and formed common bonds.
R ehabilitation started when the veil began to lift
-Arts, crafts and sports - and with
E ncouragement, I began to feel better - soon I was helping others
- as I had been helped - to get back up that slippery slope - then
A fter about six months, my veil was thrown back, like a bride at
the altar - the
K ey to future happiness and health, is to make time for yourself I was told
Then came the big day!
D ischarged to a NHS rehab centre - there I met Richard - it was
love at first sight!
O nly two weeks later, by special licence, we were
W ed! Eleven years on we lead a very happy loving life.
N o, I wasn't mad, just stressed, it was the job.

Elaine Duggan

NHS HOSPITAL

On arrival they measured me for stockings
For anti-embolism sake;
Length of leg, width of calf,
What shade or denier would I take?
My operation was planned for the next day
With a competent surgeon in command.
I have no fear when he is near,
I'm entirely in his hands.
You've done nothing all day yet you're tired,
And it's almost 10 pm.
Eyelids droop - you are drifting off -
When suddenly you are awake again.
It's the *pill* brigade with their trolley
With wheels which meander away.
But I didn't bring my WD40,
And I doubt if it would work with hairspray.
The lady in the corner was *active*
Particularly every hour of the night,
When she rearranged her locker
And banged and clattered with delight.
She trailed her catheter like a puppy
Dragging it behind by the tube;
She hated Blackpool, TV, and plants
But we said nothing, we didn't like to be rude.
The food was good, the nurses kind -
The surgeons do so well.
So thank you NHS hospital
I'll try not to return, but you never can tell!

Val Patten

ACCIDENT PRONE

They took my adenoids when I was seven, I knew if I died
I'd go to heaven,
They plastered my right wrist when I was ten, I'd chipped the bone by
falling again.
They plastered the left one, the very next week, I was accident prone
and in my peak.

They told me I had nodules when I was nineteen,
my vocal cords had to rest, no shouting or singing
no hot curries, no alcohol, no laughing and no talking at all!
They stuck things in my throat to look at the cords.
They moved me around from ward to ward.
The nodules disappeared, I was glad I had persevered.

They stole my tonsils when I was twenty,
I'll tell you this, it hurt me plenty.
The other girls cried with pain refusing to eat, driving the nurses insane.
Four weeks it took me to recover, trying hard not to cry for my mother.

Finally they got my foot, ripped to shreds, the blood did shoot.
Somehow the older you get the worse it sounds
sever laceration but no fractures found!
Twenty one and stitched six times
pride hurt, nerves shattered, is my bike lying in tatters?

Just bad luck or accident prone? Thank you for hearing me moan.
Okay so sympathy isn't always included and sometimes they can
be bad-mooded but think hard about their job
surrounded by pain misery and fear
day after day, year after year.
Doctors, nurses, surgeons and porters, they all work hard
but do we sympathise with them?

Think I'll send a *thank you card.*

S McLaughlin

A SPECIAL TEAM

That dinky cap so crisp a fold,
The dresses clean, so smart and white,
On some so young and many old,
Each aim the same in the fight.

The busy tasks though large or small
Are done so willing throughout the night,
Control may waver and spirits fall
But always humour not far from sight.

The thoughtfulness from knowledge show
With tender loving care to all,
Forever learning and keen to know
New ways to ease when pain does call.

The different fields that illness takes
The nurse must cope in every one,
Just one of many, but each to make
A special team that place to run.

The feelings all so carefully hidden
Tight is the rein on emotions raw,
Yet care she does for the bedridden,
The best to give . . . an unwritten law.

Kathleen Thornton

UNTITLED

Not everyone who suffers ill
regains good health by taking pills
or potions of the usual sort,
no, though much evidence is brought,
and claims exceptional and grand
are made to tempt the doctor's hand
who, scribbling on prescription pad
desires swift cure for lass or lad.
(Good hearted soul is taken in
by advert with seductive grin).

Now basis of a healthy nation
must stem from positive foundation
just as within the mother's womb
the infant feels himself at home
when nourished with some decent meals;
if he gets junk, disease prevails.

Likewise when the poisonous weed
chokes mum and dad, so will feed
that precious infant's cells and blood
Our NHS can do no good.

What of parents, old 'uns too
There's something that we all can do -
Keep walking, swimming, get on yer bike!
That's what the bones and muscles like.

There's something politicians must
effect to gain the people's trust . . .
Provide some housing of a kind
where kids can grow and never mind
they are not rich. They can be proud.
Where man's respected, hope's allowed.

Barbara Maskens

CHAIN OF ASSISTANCE

A patient called to a junior nurse
'Nurse I have this terrible pain!'

She says 'Wait a minute, I will ask a senior nurse'
The junior nurse tells the senior nurse about the pain

She says 'Wait a moment, I will ask Sister'
The senior nurse asks Sister about the pain

She says 'Wait a moment, I will ask the doctor'
Sister tells the doctor about the pain

He says 'Wait a moment and I will ask the surgeon'
The doctor tells the surgeon about the pain

He says 'Wait a moment and I will ask God'

Pauline Hamblin

TIME'S UP

Doctor diagnoses cancer; visit only five days past
Hospital appointment made and taken,
NHS administration fast.
Start the treatment not so pleasant
Like poison running through the veins
Side effects of sickness, baldness,
Wonder if it's worth the pain.

Admittance pending, stomach churning,
Now that operation's near,
Camaraderie with fellow patients
Scanning faces set in fear.
Nil by mouth . . . so thirsty, the drip sleep
Numbness, comforting deep.
With calming voice, the nurses linger,
Clutching wrist, pulse future finger.

Relief and gladness now it's over
Cause of pain now been and gone,
Angel nurses reassuring,
Assist with wound, such kindly deeds,
Bid farewell to mended patient
NHS efficient speed.

Jane Darnell

AN ODE TO HDC SITTING FOR SRN

The years flit by . . . oh gosh! . . . And then . . .
'Tis time to sit for SRN
You read your paper,
Your heart then sank,
You haven't the foggiest,
Your mind's a blank.
But cheer up, old dear . . .
'Ignorance is sublime'
There'll always be . . . another time.

For if the questions you mix and bungle,
I guess . . . *they* won't worry out in the jungle,
An 'ungry ca*nnibal* won't worry about SRN
As long as you're not all bones and skin!
But as you are doing *your best* old duck,
We all wish you the best of British luck!

Daisie Cecil-Clarke

WAITING

Stand in line at the window, waiting for your turn
casualty reception, a five minute interrogation you earn.
If you'd like to go to the waiting room, take a seat
where magazines lurk from years gone by, stacked so neat.
As people come and go, waiting for your name to be called
emergencies take preference, you're not being stalled.
The minute hand workman-like makes its way
ticking away the waiting hours of another day.
A nurse pops in, your name announced, follow me
what have we here? Let's have a look and see.
A cursory glance, preliminary treatment, have another seat
waiting patiently, hoping it's worthwhile when you finally meet.
Look at your watch to see how the time is flying
at least the bleeding's stopped as you wait, you could be dying.
Smiling angel beckons, the doctor will see you now
quick impersonal touch, diagnosis declared, but how
mere seconds have passed since you entered his room
now you are back waiting in the corridor's gloom.
Busy nurse appears, to bandage your wound for you
the waiting is over, there's nothing left to do.
Visit the window for a return appointment, you can hardly wait
rush home to grab some dinner, now you are running late.

Paul Birkitt

OPERATION WELFARE

Chirpy characters push the trolley
The ceiling his only sight
Head covered with a frilly hat
Trembling at his forthcoming plight.

Sympathetic nurses smiling warmly
Reassuring him of his vital operation
Guiding him toward the anaesthetic room
Doctors marking the tender location.

Attentive surgeons perform with accuracy
Capable nurses assist with speed
Swabs lined up for inspection
Available in case he should bleed

Pinned to a tailor's perfection
The painful expression faded fast
Proud of his obvious dilemma
As everyone willingly signed his plaster cast.

Jane Cook

MY BROKEN ANKLE

I broke my ankle as I ran down the hill,
the pain I felt made me feel quite ill.
Two hours from the nearest casualty unit,
my friends and I had a long time to wait.
My leg swelled up like a party balloon,
I cried so hard I felt like a fool.
Once there I was seen by the triage nurse,
I stupidly thought I'd be home in a hearse.

They X-rayed me and played with my foot,
they wheeled me around for the doctors to look.
Plastered from my knee to my toe,
with a funky pair of crutches and no place to go.
The nurses were nice they really looked after me,
they gave me painkillers which I washed down with tea.
A taxi was called and I was soon on my way,
homeward bound for a recuperation stay.

Jane Woolley

HELPLESS

I fear your babe won't live the night
You'd better come right away
He wants your blessing to give up the fight
Will you hold him, tell him it's OK
He's struggled hard to stay in this world
You love him and he knows it well.
But he's going soon
He just can't hold on
Please come.

The nurse hung up the phone
She wept alone
'Please come,' she muttered into the air,
to the worst pain you'll ever bear.
I'll sit you down in a comfy chair
and having switched off all alarms
I'll lift your dying baby to your arms
And, impotent, I'll watch you there.
Your heart will be broken
With grief that can't be spoken.
And I won't be able to help.

Is this how you feel, God, when seeing our pain?
I'll see only one mother's baby die today
But you'll see them all, and all the time.
Yes, He sees them all, but one at a time.
And He's not only the nurse, watching with tear-stained eyes
He's the helpless parent as well, holding His son while he dies.

C J Sykes

NO ANGEL

Up in the morning out in the rain
Why do I do this again and again
A car that won't start because the weather's so cold
Oh I know why I do this, one day I will be old
I knock on the door or ring on the bell
Wait patiently I say, you know she's not well
She opens the door and there on her face
Are years full of memories time can't erase.
I'm so glad you've come she says so sincere
Come in and sit down, have some tea my dear
I've had a bad night and sleep would not come
It got so bad I wished the Lord would take me home
I look at her face and a tear starts to fall
You're an angel she says.
No just a district nurse that's all.

Sally Watson

HOW TO BEHAVE IN HOSPITAL

Our NHS hospitals are much maligned,
My experience has been of a different kind.
Three times in twelve months I had to go
Under the surgeon's knife, so I should know.
The doctors and nurses are just great;
The food in my view is first rate.
The wards are decorated in lovely hues,
Guaranteed to keep away the blues.
Now a few rules you must observe,
Don't be frightened, don't lose your nerve.
When on the examination couch you're supine,
And the doc's got his hand 'where the sun don't shine',
Relax, think of England, don't you fret,
You ain't seen nothing yet!
When the nurse comes towards you with a cheeky grin,
And says 'time to have your enema in.'
Don't turn pale and shake with fright,
It'll be gone before the end of night!
Now's the time for false teeth to come out,
Do not yell and do not shout,
Just hand them meekly to the nice nurse,
And don't you fume and don't you curse.
The day arrives for stitches to come out,
Now remember not to fuss and shout.
Lie back and display 'true British Grit'
And with the nurses you'll be a hit.
Now when all is said and done,
I wish to say thanks to each and everyone
Of the doctors and nurses who take such care,
To ensure our stay in hospital is beyond compare.

Dorothy Schofield

HOSPITAL DRAMA

If you're on the NHS, it seems that they couldn't care less
that is why it's often left too late
If you're hoping for a bed, you could end up nearly dead
your illness was so bad you couldn't wait

It's hell waiting for an operation where there is no ultimation
and you know the outcome in advance
The surgeon gives you an examination, notifies administration
and whispers that you have a fifty, fifty chance

In six months' time you get a letter, although you may be feeling better
you suddenly end up in a panic
You write in reply to say, that now you're feeling quite okay
and make another appointment for the clinic

There you are lying in bed with a sign above your head
on it 'Nil by mouth'
You're feeling rather dumb in the area of your bum
where the nurse has acted most uncouth

You come around and start to rage, tongue like the bottom of a parrot cage
you're feeling sore and ill at ease
A nurse comes over she looks very nice, your head is in a metal vice
and some sadist is giving it a squeeze

The surgeon comes into the ward, from the end of the bed he takes
the clipboard
and says your illness has got us all beat
I meant to remove your big toe, which was causing you such woe
but I've inadvertently taken off both your feet

Now don't you fret, for there's much more to come yet
wait until I tell you the good news
A patient of mine down in ward ten has learnt to walk all over again
so I sold him your new leather shoes

Next time that you are waiting for a bed, don't get upset and worry your head
just bide your time and see how long it takes
The surgeon doesn't worry if you're not admitted in a hurry
for after all he can bury his mistakes

Billy Bale

DELYTH WARD

To the staff of Delyth Ward,
Thank you for all your care.
When we felt so poorly,
We knew that you'd be there
When you came with a needle,
You were so very kind,
Gave us a nice smile,
To take things off our mind.
Some of the jobs you are given
Must be hard for you.
Putting up with us grumbling,
When you're such a happy crew.
The housekeepers cleaned,
And gave us cups of tea.
To see you all so busy,
Your hard work for all to see.
If all hospital wards
Were as good as this,
We wouldn't mind being in hospital
If we couldn't give it a miss.

Josie Minton

WELCOME TO THE THEATRE

Come on in, you won't be long,
we operate with a happy song.
The sheets are clean, the beds are soft,
the service is free you can keep your cash.
Now just slip into this nicely starched one-piece dress
and take yourself a well-earned rest.
We'll tie this tag upon your wrist,
oh what's your religion, don't say atheist.
The consultant's here with his fledgling team,
they've come to gloat, he'll make you scream.
Don't worry son I've done this before,
I've lacerated many a skin pour.
These new technologies may be here to stay,
the magic eye I hear you say,
with these new-fangle gadgets
I'm not too clever
they come and go like the changing weather.
But place a scalpel in my palm
and I'll be right in, you'll come to no harm,
just a scar it's my calling card,
you can show your friends your Mum and Dad.
The porter's here you're on your way,
we all hope that you enjoyed your stay.
Now where's that vein and count to five
you'll be comatosed but still alive.
Welcome to the recovery room,
you look in pain but we'll relieve that soon,
a shot of morphine should do the trick,
happy dreams hope you're not sick.

Gareth Thomas

NURSING IN 1947

The interview went well at the major London hospital,
They were selective so I must await my call,
Salary was not mentioned, money was of no consideration
Nursing was a vocation.

Seven thirty, making beds. Learning cases as we went along,
Damp dusting, polishing, by nine am the long ward shone.
Beds well made with wheels set straight but faults were found
On sister's round.

Decorum must always be observed, dresses well below the knee,
Long butterfly caps, no make-up allowed or jewellery,
A stiff starched apron and collar chafing our skin
We suffered in.

We worked 'til nine, with meals and just a two hour break
Which, if the ward could spare us, we asked permission to take.
Study lectures dictated how our break we'd often spend.
We must attend.

Seniority was important too, no speaking unless spoken to,
And orders unquestionably obeyed if senior to you.
The smallest misdemeanour ended with regret
On matron's carpet.

We could not wear a cardigan even though the wind was chilling
And for every thermometer we broke we were fined one shilling.
We must be in by half past ten, lights out by eleven.
Breakfast compulsory - at seven.

We learned much more than just professional excellence,
We learned patience, humility, selflessness and tolerance,
To appreciate the simple things like putting up one's feet.
That life is sweet.

Hilda M Norden

HEALING HANDS

Within those walls are healing hands
giving succour allaying fear,
pain and suffering understand
of patients there within their care.

Soothing now the fevered brow
or temperature and pulse to take,
these are hands that show us how
when duty calls will ne'er forsake.

I pray the day when patients find
health restored and will to roam,
happiness and peace of mind
in the place that they call home.

William Fisher

FAILING PATIENT

'I'm so afraid,' you say
'and so sad'
Your quivering hand reaches out,
Trembling and pitifully beseeching,
Tearing at my heart,
Wringing me with sympathy.

'I have no-one, they're all gone.
No-one to love me, care for me,
Really care . . . I want to die.'
Shivering, wrinkled form with frightened soul,
Take my hand, accept some comfort
From this passenger on life's journey.

See the sky, the sun, the rain,
The flowers, the night, the day;
All your friends and still here.
You will have warmth and food
No need for fear,
And gentle tending hands
When death draws near.

Pauline Boncey

VOLUNTEERS

V oid perhaps our lives would be,
O ther's needs we try to see,
L ove and care, a crutch we give,
U naware how some folks live,
N eeding time we're free to heed
T he little things patients need,
E ver thankful we are here,
E xpress our thanks life is dear,
R eassure just take their hand,
S imply try to understand.

Suzanne Joy Golding

D O P

Panic, panic, fearful panic,
I know again I'm going manic.
O help, hell's bells and knicker legs
It'll be the DOP and dried up scrambled eggs.
No more fun now everyone's gone
All there'll be will be me and my neurone.
It's Latin for nerve but I won't care
As all I'll be fit for is to sit and stare.
The DOP is alright, I suppose.
But it's not exactly what I'd have 'choose'.
A simple chair with a telly in the corner
They don't ever have a simple sauna.
And that padded cell makes me all a jitter
The ECT turns you into a fritter.
So when all is said and done
The DOP just ain't no fun.
There's all those drugs they make you take
Which just as you get your tea they make you shake.
It's no fun being mentally ill
All it is, is pill after pill.
The nurses don't smile from morn 'til night,
O well blow them all, where's my gelignite?
O good, no more fear, no more panic
No longer am I diagnosed as manic.
Where's the DOP? O it's gone too
What's that I see? Ah yes! The sky is blue.

Denise Shaw

LIFE IS SO MUCH BETTER NOW

So used to being in command of the situation
It came as a shock
When my own health deteriorated.
I had to be the patient and be looked after,
the rules suddenly and surely reversed.
I have to take my life in the slow lane
and enjoy each day and not watch the clock.
No running after others at their beck and call.
It's my turn to be spoilt,
and they can go and pick themselves up after a fall.
So used to being in command of the situation.
I let them take over the helm.
Life is so much better now
and I'm recovering well.
I take joy in the little things
I had no time to notice before.
I write letters now and have lots of news to tell.
The tall trees that bend and sway across the sky
and the lovely perfume of the flowers.
I am so lucky and have a beautiful store,
so used to being in command of the situation.
I now sit back and let them take control
and when the tea is offered
I say yes please, is there any more?

Rosemary Medland

FIVE HOURS TO SPARE?

I arrived at the hospital without delay
Yet still I've sat for most of the day
I rushed around to be on time
My appointment being half past nine
Here I'm sitting at half past twelve
I open my bag and in I delve
Alas nothing to eat and nothing to drink
I heave a sigh and then I think
Of a bright idea, it's worth a try
So I walked to the desk and began to cry
'I'm feeling faint my injection is due
Could I possibly go to the front of the queue'
But a patient heard me boy she flew
'What may I ask is special about you'
'Nothing' I said as I crawled back to my seat
Lord, I wish I had something to eat
'Nothing' I wish I had something to eat
It's now two o'clock and they've called my name
I go to get up but I think I've gone lame
I'm as stiff as a board my bones are cracking
Those little chairs have done my back in
The doctor had no time to chat
I was in and out in two minutes flat
'How are you today' he'd said with a frown
'I have felt better' I said sitting down
There was no answer as he flicked through my file
I twiddled my thumbs and after a while
He decided with treatment I should be fine
'So come back next month at half past nine'
I thought 'you'll be lucky I'll make you wait
I'll have a lie in and arrive very late.'

Barbara Ramsey

GLANDULAR FERVOUR

I'm prostrate with my prostate,
I'm in a gloomy ward,
However, thanks to NHS,
I'm anything but bored

I *think* this drink is coffee,
The Hoover starts its din,
Wallop, crash, they're moving beds,
To squeeze more punters in

Old Charlie (op tomorrow),
Is having crafty smoke,
And Fred, who's got a hernia,
Tells nurse a dirty joke

The night shift's handing over
To day shift, what a maul!
They're putting him who snores a lot,
In side-ward down the hall

The Social Worker's busy,
She looks like Sec of State,
You know, Virginia Bottomley,
The Lottery-lover's mate

The occupational therapist
Is drumming up some trade,
She's got that navvy knitting,
And me? - I'm weaving braid!

The vicar and the priest are here,
And so's the Pentecostals,
And someone's selling little books
In aid of homeless hostels!

Now people have their jobs to do,
I don't want to condemn,
But the ward's like Piccadilly,
And it's only 7am!!

Peter Davies

THE NHS EXPERIENCE

'If' when you are ill, with us you have to stay
Let us help to brighten your day
Pills and potions will help you get well,
So do the Surgeons, Doctors and Nurses as well
Porters, Cleaners, Secretaries all have jobs to do
All indirectly involved just for you
There are beds to make, forms to fill
A clean water glass for your pill
Linen to launder, pressed like new;
All to be done for the visit by you
Meals to prepare three times a day
We all work hard to earn our pay
Just as you wake to begin your day new,
Breakfast we gladly prepare for you
A few hours later lunch is made
All served on trays neatly laid
Meat and two veg is on the menu today
Sent up to the wards, no sign of delay
Choices of sweets, What decision to make
Milk pudding, ice cream or a fancy cake
Pots to wash, trays to clear
You don't get to see us but we're all here
Working hard behind the scenes
We're the staff who, cooks washes and cleans
At the end of the day we all do our best
Along with the Doctors, Nurses and the rest
We try to help you have a pleasant stay
And hope you get well without delay
Get well soon with our best wishes.
From the catering dept; who washes your dishes.

Yvonne Monks

PICKET ON THE NHS

At the entrance road to the hospital
I saw pickets with placards one day
I wanted to join them and asked what to do
Perhaps I could help in some way

Someone informed me shout scabs dirty scabs
And just wave this banner all day
I soon got myself in a frenzy
Suppose I got carried away

I screamed votes for nurses, burn your bras
Everybody out
Then a nurse whispered it's about more work
But they won't dish more money out

So I shouted scabs dirty scabs
Get your money out
Scabs dirty scabs
We're not going to nurse 'em for nowt

Everyone chanted scabs dirty scabs
And the tempo started to rise
Scabs dirty scabs
They had a glazed look in their eyes

Scabs dirty scabs
I had them all marching around
Scabs dirty scabs
How could I calm them down

Scabs dirty scabs
They were smashing up the place
Scabs dirty scabs
I got out of there with haste.

Fred Tighe

YOU DROPPED A GAFFE NHS

Oh what a traumatic experience oh what an NHS
They sent me to a hospital to take pictures
of my chest. Why are we waiting, the queue
was incredibly long, a white coated worker came
up to me and said broken bone but I could
be wrong, he went away, and it was in the
next bay, I had to change into a gown,
A sister who spoke, said we looked at the book
we are expecting you, you know, trouble is papers
have gone amiss and the doctor's gone into town
Eventually I was in front of a long chute
and got the needle only it was in my tired
back, they slid me into this long chute
left the room and didn't come back

A long time elapsed and I was still trapped
I yelled at the top of my voice,
finally a man came in and said are you
still here Mr Price I'll take these plates and
send you home it can't have been very nice.

David Price

THE NHS - CARE IN THE COMMUNITY

As we turn the corners of the mind
Ever decreasing circles of consciousness to find
They say we are out of sync
But we are just the sensitive ones
Responding to a world on the brink
        The Asylum walls
        Are now trees oh so small
For we are now in a period of transition
        Of Community care
        Of indecision
We rely on a daily intake of pills
The system answers to all our ills
But for the root cause
The labyrinth of despair
There is no hope out there.

Finnan Boyle

PSST . . . HEARD THE ONE ABOUT THE NHS?

Mrs Mac. had a bad back and problems with her knees
The GP said 'Get plenty of rest, for the pain, please take these.'
He wrote off to the hospital, Mrs Mac. went home to wait
For the postman to bring confirmation of her appointment date.
While Mrs Mac. waited, with some trepidation,
She took her pills which among other things, gave her constipation,
But, being of the opinion that burdens are lessened by smiles
She refused to be downhearted despite constipation causing piles!
Meanwhile, due to the tightening of the strings on the Government purse,
Problems within the NHS were getting considerably worse
And poor Mrs Mac's wait for diagnosis was to drag on three whole years,
Often, finding it hard to smile, she ended up in tears.
The GP said 'Mrs Mac. I am of the impression
This has all got too much, you now suffer from depression.'
Very kindly he tried to help and said 'Things will ease
If you go home, rest and take eight a day of these'
Mrs Mac. refused the pills, she did this quite politely
Thanked him for his efforts, all the time smiling . . . *Tightly*!
She realises his hands are tied and he's doing all he can
But he's no magician, he's just an ordinary man.
And things are forever changing, these problems will not last
Soon they will just be a memory, in the dim and distant past.
Readers are advised that Mrs Mac. should not be lamented
Her face has regained its smile, albeit slightly demented!

Sue McShera

NURSE CHRISTINA

And as I laid in the sanctuary
Hiding and broken in spirit,
Like a candle in the night
Her face glowing white as snow
And soft, tender, searching eyes,
Like a moving silent host
Her hands mopped my fevered brow,
Now feeling healed and blessed
My tired eyes took their rest,
A veiled dream did pursue,
Of a choir of angels singing too
And a white cathedral in the night
Giving me the kiss of life,
As I wandered on a road
A strange woman came my way
With a white stick on a silver tray,
As the light came in through the window pane
I awoke to the sound of thunder
And her voice spoke in gentle tones,
Dear, here's something for your hunger
Milk, fish and bread on my bed,
I stood and gazed and wondered
About that fateful day when I lost my way,
When the black cloud followed by
The stormy waves came from afar
And suicide shone in the stars,
Our Holy Father loving mercy
Feeling Christina's loving gaze
Thank you, Nurse Christina rose
I will always love and remember you.

Thomas Hull

HOME AT LAST

(Waiting for the ambulance to come to go home after a long stay in hospital)

The waiting time is painful -
each moment the length of four.
Waiting in the hospital ward.
longing to get out of the door.

Nothing could go wrong, could it?
They wouldn't change their mind
and leave me here for ever -
the patient they kept behind.

Each moment lasts the time of four,
yet the minute hand creeps on.
It's not that the staff aren't super,
it's just that I'd rather be gone!

Janis Priestley

LADIES ONLY

Heaven protect me and save me oh Lord
I'm now on the gynaecological ward.
Nurses are busily shaving and clipping.
Surgeons are expertly cutting and snipping,
Removing and tying, stitching and scraping.
Anaesthetised women, who dream of escaping.

Nurse speaks to deaf lady, stressing the vowels.
'Have you passed water and how are the bowels?
And pop this thermometer under your tongue.
I'll check your blood pressure, it doesn't take long.
I've got to slow down, I'll be needing a head scan.
Speak up now, does anyone else want a bed pan?'

Middle aged lady awaits Hysterectomy,
It's sterilisation for the younger one next to me.
There's fibroids, polyps, and things I can't mention,
Like post operative wind, and water retention.
There's lots of discomfort a little amazement,
At various treatments, like hormone replacement.

The indignities suffered I'd rather not tell.
They've all seen my thingies and whatsits as well.
Nothing's secret or sacred under my duvet.
I feel like the star of a dreadful blue movie.
Heaven protect me and save me Amen.
It'll be as a man, if I come back again.

Olive Holland

EVERYBODY OUT!

Before I worked for the NHS,
Matron ruled the hospital team
With well regulated procedures,
And followed the Golden Mean.
Patients' care was the first priority:
Carers the working majority.

After Salmon Report, the changes came in.
Our *nursing officers* practised admin.,
Studied public accountability,
Project returns and viability.
Can vocation and compassion meet our needs
For each patient (five minutes) in NHS squeeze?

When people *not-yet-admitted*
See their city hospital close,
The flow becomes more efficient -
Though the tide of paperwork grows.
To solve the *In-Patients'* problem
With primary care, never doubt:

It's a smoother operation
With the patients contracted out.

Laura May

THE NURSE

They are dying,
Their lips are parted,
Their breath is shallow,
Their relatives try to fight back the tears,
To be strong
For the corpse that lays before them,
I'm a nurse, I don't cry, I help, I care, I comfort.

They are dying,
Their eyes are silent,
Their mouths speak foreign,
A dead soul in a well body,
Their relatives try to fight back the tears,
To be strong,
To be able to aid their soulless companion.
I'm a nurse, I don't cry, I give information, I give advice
I give consolement.

They are dying,
Their eyes are lively,
Their body is fit,
But their liver is weak,
And riddled with cancer, it's too late, it's spread.
Their relatives try to fight back the tears,
To be strong,
To allow their friend's last days to be great,
I'm a nurse, I don't cry, I give medication, observe their development,
I monitor their deterioration.

I'm a nurse, I do cry, I do feel, I do hurt,
I do my job.

Claire Thomas

THREE CHEERS FOR THE NHS

If it hadn't been for the NHS
I wouldn't be here today.
The superb treatment I received
I couldn't begin to repay.

I had a major op.
Life-threatening my illness was,
But the wonderful after attention
Ensured I was snatched from death's jaws.

I'd never been in a hospital
And so was really nervous.
My fears were soon overcome -
The kindness was just tremendous.

After my quick recovery
I was sent to convalesce
In another large hospital
Where the attention was again a success.

Here female beds were scarce,
So two of us were asked to go
To a room off the male ward,
And we didn't like to say no.

We had our private shower
Though the men's dayroom we used
For meals and watching TV,
And the men were politely amused.

In both of those big hospitals
I was treated like a princess,
And I was more than satisfied
With our much maligned NHS.

Helena Kerr

THE NATIONAL ELF SERVICE

Get up we need to make your bed,
the smiling uniformed Lady said.
I looked at the drip and catheter too,
how could I move I had not a clue.

So with catheter held and saline drip,
I stood up praying I would not loose my grip.
Then back into bed where I fell asleep,
to be woken by Doctor, from a slumber deep.

He said I was fine and doing my best,
but to try hard to get plenty of rest.
So I had my lunch then my tea and a drink,
and back to bed after a wash in the sink.

I woke at midnight, the ward stood still,
I saw an orange haired lady with my pill.
Who are you I asked with a disbelieving voice,
I'm the nurse who's helping out by choice.

Your nurses are so busy that is why we are here,
to help, to make you better, you see my dear.
So do not be alarmed, my name is Fergus,
and I work for The National Elf Service!

Jil Bramhall

THE NHS EXPERIENCE

My opinion of hospitals' services, at this present time
is going down hill,
The waiting lists are terrible, for one who is ill,
By the time a patient arrives at a hospital, one could get worse
Hospitals are just closing down, and the departure of a nurse.

Whatever is going on, whatever will the system think of next
in this country,
All I have thoughts for, the community is not run properly,

Myself, around about 20 years ago, I was in a NHS hospital,
Nurses and doctors couldn't do enough for me, and others I recall,
I was actually on my last breath, they thought I was at death's door,
But, with one prayer to God, another prayer was answered, once more.

With good attention, I survived, but, then the doctors and nurses
had time to spare
No rushing around, plenty of beds empty, and more care,
Even in those times, of about 20 years past, just women were
in wards together,
Men were in their own wards, more privacy altogether,
There was no mixed wards, as it is seen of today,
Not such a bundle, as it now appears in this way,

Whatever is going on, with these hospitals closing.
Even if a person is in dreadful pain, there seems to be weeks of waiting,
By then, the pains may be gone, or a patient may die,
Whichever way we turn, we will never know why,

Does the Government really care for this community,
For these hospitals that are closing one by one, or the staff
is short, as we can see
Whenever doctors or nurses ask for a well-deserved pay rise
Whatever happens, there is a war and cry, for just a price.

If ever the Government do just get together, to know what is going on,
I am sure they can all come to a conclusion, and help the hospitals along,
So there will be none of this pointless matter.
As I am still here to tell the tale, when there were more services
working then for the better.

J McGovern

DAY SURGERY

I'm sitting in bed in a hospital ward,
I haven't been here very long.
I know I'll be home for tea tonight
for there's nothing really wrong.

Although it's really very nice here
and there's carpets on the floor,
lovely pictures and a comfy bed,
I'd rather be going through the door.

I've had a chat with the 'gas' man
and the surgeon's sharpened his knife,
I'm beginning to change my mind
even though this will change my life.

I'm lying on the trolley now
surrounded by wires and people in blue,
there's a cold, heavy feeling by my elbow
then the room disappears from view.

All of a sudden my eyes are open,
I think they've made a mistake
they don't seem to have operated just yet -
goodness, what is that terrible ache?

I'm sitting back in bed now,
a lovely nurse is giving me tea,
the other patients are smiling broadly
and I feel like royalty.

This is no Nuffield hospital
or a clinic in the best end of town,
this is the good old NHS
so don't you dare put it down!

Cecilia Saunders

A PATIENT IN THE NATIONAL HEALTH SERVICE

Although I nursed in the National Health
I'm afraid I'm apt to treat it with stealth.
But recently I spent a few days there,
And I saw very few that really care.

Life gets more and more like office work,
No wonder there are so many who would rather shirk.
Admittedly they know their stuff,
But when it comes to the practicable, the going gets tough.

The patient no longer comes first - as it did in my day,
Whilst a muddle is sorted through they must in agony lay,
Instead of letting more patients face their fate.
Get nurses back to the bedside before it's too late.

In the end I asked if I could go home,
I'd recover far more quickly in the quiet and alone.
The doctor agreed and arranged it for that day,
And very soon I was on my way.

Betty Green

NHS

The NHS was started for the people we were told,
But setting up of Management's soon caused a stranglehold.
Now patients have to bear their pain while waiting for the call,
Having an op or treatment takes second place that's all.

Age makes a difference, if you're old I'm afraid, you go to the end of the queue.
Some never live for their operation date, it could be me or you!
What is the Government doing? People don't count as before.
If only they saw the suffering they cause,
we're too tired to complain anymore.

No beds for the patients, nor Nurse to be trained,
ICU needs specialised staff.
Money is short for treatment,
Only Management gets the cash.

So all you Management staff look out,
When NHS comes to a halt,
You won't have jobs, then you'll know what it's like
To be second class citizens, whose fault?

A Pincombe

INTENSIVE CARE

Telephone. Wails and sirens.
Emergency - urgency.
Tassel of tubes. Monitors meter
Those rough coughs. Moans - groans.

Higher knowledge. Pulsating energy.
Low life ebbs. Blood - needles - vomit.
Swabs. The pulse of technology
Competes with that mask of eternity.

Bleep - bleep. Keep on that heart-beat.
Calm staff respond. A supreme feat
To sustain life. Busy silent feet
Hurry over cushioned sterile floor to beat
Death.

Wealth and stealth
of supreme surgeon's skills
guided by the healing knife
of whom? But, I know, I saw a saved life!

R Peter Smith

NATIONAL HEALTH SERVICE

If you are troubled with a bad back
There's a waiting list to see the Quack
Years and years you will have to wait
Just to get an X-ray plate
All National Health beds are full
Hospital food's completely dull
All that waiting time you spent
Just to see an Asian Gent
Consultant's sure to get his fee
From an overworked tax payer like me.

F A Rawlinson

NO POWER, NO GLORY

The family are gathered round the bed,
It's your duty to tell them their beloved is dead.
The day and date, the time and cause,
This responsibility is yours.
You're given all the menial tasks,
From day to day you're always asked
To make the beds and pour the tea,
But when it comes to a tragedy
An important position is given to you
When there's a job no-one else wants to do.
No diagnosis can you give,
However when they want to know how long they'll live:
'We'll get the nurse to give the reply,
We don't want to tell you when you'll die.'
Then the next moment you're folding blankets again,
You can't prescribe pills to ease the pain.
Those in power take all the glory
But when there's bad news it's a different story.
Working the wards is an awful curse,
That's why I'm no longer an NHS nurse.

Kathy Lovett

DOCTORS AND THAT PEN

The NHS is not very good
I'd stay away from doctors, if only I could
I suffer from bronchitis, so I'm often there
But they never listen to me,
            They just don't care
I had post-natal depression, 10 years ago
when I went to my doctor,
            he didn't want to know
Just women's problems
            that's what he said
but I felt like hell, and that soon I'd be dead
So I found a new doctor
            that's what I did then
he listened and talked a little
            then took out his pen
loads of pills I was given
            so that I would sleep
because up to that point
            I'd just weep and weep
I started to get better, a little each day
back to normal and feeling OK
but now 10 years later
            this doctor's the same
it takes all his time even
to remember my name
I suppose if you're lucky
a good one, you could get
if only I could
            as I haven't found one yet.

Heather Dunn-Fox from Leek

FRED'S NEW HIP

When you have an operation it's quite a trying time
Are your smalls all clean and white, and have you left some on the line?
Do your socks have any holes and are your feet quite clean
Will they see that funny mole or will it get by them unseen?

What sort of Nurses will be there to handle all your parts
To lift you up and turn you round amidst the fits and starts
'Twill be your luck, just wait and see, to get a dishy Nurse
Your embarrassment you'll have to hide as you try not to curse.

Your blood pressure will shoot right up and they'll say, 'Sorry Fred
Unless it comes right down again, we'll do your mate instead.'
And all the while that rubber sheet is creeping up your back
The bed feels like a plank of wood, the sheets are rough and slack.

'Now Frederick' says that dishy Nurse, 'you really must keep still.
Have you opened up your bowels today, if not you'll need a pill.
I'm coming back this afternoon to start and get you ready
The razor's blunt, we do it dry, but my hand is nice and steady.'

'Lie back and think of England Fred' said the young Nurse with a smile
'This job of yours is quite complex and could take quite a while.
I'll try some gentle massage which should keep you cool and calm.'
And so she fetched the baby cream and put some in her palm.

Poor Fred, he reconciled himself, 'cos he could do no other
He wondered how a brand new hip could have caused him so much bother
And as the Nurse's creamy hands with love and care rubbed lightly
His thoughts then strayed to far off days when he was young and carefree.

If this was having a brand new hip then her therapy was working
He thought 'I'll have the other one done and not once think of shirking.'
And so our hero, brave and true, not once was he found lacking
They did the job and stitched him up and then they sent him packing.

Shirley Whiles

THE NHS IS DEAD

We can all remember the days when
a visit to the Doctor, gave us hope to believe
that we would soon be well again.
We had confidence in medical prowess
but today, that is all but gone,
today we are lucky if the Doctor looks up
whenever we enter his room,
Blood pressure is not routinely checked,
and ill defined pain goes unexamined
A prescription for a disease vaguely diagnosed,
is that all we can hope for in these 'enlightened days'?
How many poor souls will have to die?
Before those in power see what is awry.
Doctors now are called upon to value human life,
who is to live and who will sadly die
How hard a task, to play at being God,
who'll be called and who'll be left
is determined by what we can offer mankind
alternatively the riches in the bank
can be the means of our recovery
and the poor go to the wall.
What has happened to our health service?
the same service for rich and poor!
We can't rely on our health service any more!

Elisabeth James

MY TIME AS A PATIENT - HOSPITALS NOW

I was a glutton and ate with a terrible greed.
My goitre had rapidly grown and I had to concede,
That a throat operation had been my desperate need.

The hospital floors disinfectantly washed, were polished and gleaming.
Food came to us on trays, delicious and steaming.
It was better than I thought, and I thought I'd been dreaming.

But then came the day when I was wheeled on a trestle
And confronted by an anaesthetist I wanted to wrestle,
Until he stuck a sharp needle into my vessel.

I went out like a light and next day I felt sore.
I was awfully sick and it splashed on the floor
And I could not look up to the ceiling no more.

My neck was painted in blue brimstone and did look a sight
And there were several clips and they felt rather tight.
But determined to recover, I put up a fight.

As slowly the days passed, the clips were removed
And the scar started healing in a neat little groove
And then out of bed I was able to move.

Back home, relatives told me the scar had looked very fine.
It looked like a necklace, a crease, not a line.
When I looked in the mirror, there was hardly a sign.

Today, hospitals are carpeted and modern, not quaint.
They don't smell of antiseptic, disinfectant but maybe paint.
With floors grandly carpeted in which you could faint.

The smart nurses uniforms no longer exist,
Still, caps were quite starchy, so may not be missed.
And the blood bank's so red that Dracula cannot resist!
So in writing about the NHS I will desist.

Henrietta Lee

MY MIRACLE

It hardly seems a year ago
The little boy I got to know
A dramatic entrance was your birth
A little miracle came to earth

'Let him be alive' is what I said
As I bled and bled upon that bed
The commotion that went on around
The screams inside my head were bound

And Daddy held you close that night
As you came out with such a fight
And he put you to my face I cried
I do not remember although I tried

Four days on I felt so weak
But I put my face close to your cheek
My love for you was strong and true
You looked at me as if you knew

The doctors the midwives fought for me
And you were as strong as can be
They told daddy that I could die
I could not hear him say 'But why but why?'

They cared for me and made me strong
They worked so hard and hours so long
A nurse she stayed close by my side
As you looked at me eyes open wide

I felt so ill and I was so weak
I could look at you but could not speak
A special hospital saved my life
Gave Daddy you and he kept his wife

My little man you are growing fast
Your baby days don't seem to last
And one year on you are my pride my joy
Thank God for Miracles, my baby boy.

Lannette Lusk

A TRIP TO THE HOSPITAL

It was about eleven o'clock last week
We were going to a big country show
Unfortunately I had a slight accident
And I was not able to go

I tripped and fell right down the stairs
In fact I took most of them on my face
I broke my nose and cut it quite badly
On my forehead I had a huge graze

My friend called an ambulance because of the blood
It arrived within three minutes
They took me to the local hospital
The cut needed some stitches in it

I had to wait for about five hours
And the reason was more or less
Everyone else seemed to have had heart attacks
Whilst my problem was not deadly, just a mess

They called down a specialist to stitch my wound
So that the scaring would be the least
It took him an hour to do ten stitches
But the job he did was really neat

I finally left there at six o'clock
Armed with appointments galore
I cannot complain at the treatment I had
Even though my nose is sore.

Sonia Gillings

JIMMY'S IS NUMBER ONE

My daughter was two; she had collapsed at home,
So I got the doctor on the telephone,
He then came straight away to see what was wrong,
He then said that it was hospital that she did belong.
She had to have a lumber puncture inside her spine,
'Please tell me what is wrong with this child of mine.'
Her skin was so pale it was so grey,
And she was so well when she was playing today.
Her eyes then rolled into the back of her head,
I screamed with fear I thought that she was dead.
The way the doctors looked I knew she was ill,
Then I did pray for her life with all of my will.
Baffled and confused the doctors worked on,
All the tests showed, that there was nothing they could find wrong.
A nurse was by her bed all throughout the night,
She had tubes and wires, so that my daughter could fight.
Motionless so still she laid on that bed,
I had fear and confusion locked in my head.
The doctors had worked hard and done all that they could.
The nurses were angels they treated me so good.
As morning approached my head was a blur,
But it was then that my daughter did then stir.
She then opened her eyes then began to smile,
Everyone was confused for a long while.
I then jumped up and I held her so near,
That's when all my worries started to clear.
It will always be a mystery, why she became ill,
Maybe it was my prayers that God did fulfil.
But the staff were so good they showed us such care,
And the hospital like ours we all should share.

Angie Armstrong

JUST ANOTHER DAY

I lie on the trolley -
Heart beating fast
The needle gets nearer
The chasm grows vast
The sensation of falling -
The room going round
My head starts spinning
Then I can't hear a sound.

A moment, an hour
A day of my life -
How long has it been
Since my moment of strife?
'The op is now over'
I hear a voice say
'Oh no, you are wrong -
it's the beginning today'

My new heart inside me
Beats now - strong and true
But it cost you your life
And all that you knew
How can I ever
Hope to repay
The debt that I owe you
For my life today?

Lyn Casey

WHEN WILL THEY LISTEN

I waited at reception to see the nurse as directed
To find I needn't have bothered I was expected.
How could they not see as I shuffled to the room
I couldn't walk. Companion Pain filled me with gloom.

You've brought your nightie. I looked blank. Whatever did they mean.
I thought some tablets would do the trick. I'm glad my clothes are clean.
The doctor came quite soon, I'll give him that, duplicating questions
Already asked. And Companion Pain hid its intentions.

Only when I walk. I could have said the Moon is Caerphilly cheese
For all the notice paid. I do not know. It puzzles me.
We'll have to make some tests. I'll admit you to the ward.
I'm staying in. Whatever next. Companion Pain I can't afford.

Why, I asked myself, did I give in especially on a Friday.
Far better to have rested and kept it hard at bay.
The hospital shuts down like a dry Welsh County Sunday.
Everything in obeyance. Companion Pain lays low.

Saturday I overdid things. Walked too far I guess.
I had to use the telephone. They don't believe the pain exists.
They think it's in my mind. I tell them it's only when I walk.
But thought seeds fall on barren ground. Companion Pain waits to stalk.

I had a turn. It frightened me when I returned to bed.
Blood pressure hit the ceiling. Body shaking uncontrollably.
The gift of oxygen more precious than gold. I hope they notice what I said.
I'll have to wait and see. Companion Pain hides within me.

I can't go home. It isn't wise. I guess I'll have to stay.
I have to play the waiting game unsure of what they'll say.
I sense that nothing more'll be done 'til Sunday's passed away.
I'll have to tell them once again. Companion Pain stays at bay.

Lewis Terrie

A DAY IN HOSPITAL

Weird noises all night long
The day starts before the dawn
Before you are really awake
Your temperature the nurse will take
Blood pressure next for you and me
Then it's time for a cup of tea.

The night staff rush around
trying not to make a sound
Next it's time for doctors rounds
With the students all gathered round
Will there be a result today
To bring an end to your hospital stay

Nurses, doctors and cleaners too
Seem to enjoy all they do
You have been awake for hours
Then visitors arrive with fruit and flowers
On and on the hours pass
The night staff arrive at last

The evening drinks are brought round
Tea, coffee and Horlicks is passed around
One patient says sugar please nurse
Other patients take none of course
Now you will hear someone's gentle snore
Signalling another day's over that's for sure.

Jean Bradbury

THE OUTPATIENT

Eleven o'clock exactly I was due to arrive
To find a parking space, round and round I had to drive
It's now getting late, so taking the first free spot
I dash into reception at 11.00 on the dot

The receptionist says, 'take a seat and please wait.'
So I sat down in the queue, relieved I wasn't late
As I patiently waited the next ten minutes or so
The lady next to me told me her tale of woe

Then from one of the examining rooms came a nurse dressed in blue
To inform all the patients whose appointments were due
That the Doctor was running a little bit late
So I needn't have panicked and got in a state

It seemed to be ages, then it became my turn at last
By that time at least a half an hour had passed
I was asked by the Doctor to return for more tests
Come back in three weeks was all he could suggest

So I left the hospital still not knowing what was wrong
The time on my parking ticket meant I hadn't been too long
There was a note on my car saying don't park here
Next time you'll be clamped straight away, never fear

I'd parked in the wrong place because I'd been in such a hurry
When I arrived back at work with the news, they said not to worry
So I'll go back in three weeks and hope that I'm okay
And I'll not worry or think about it until my appointment that day.

Susan Rowe

HOSPITAL FRIEND

We're now awake and contemplating the excitement of the day,
Our every need is taken care of as in our beds we lay,
Considering all the things that we can do I just hope
  that we can cope,
To just turn over will take a while, and then it's back
  again, we hope.
It's getting more interesting by the minute, if only we
  can stand the pace.
We'll soon be on our way to the showers and toilets, a
  kind of gentle race,
There's the humorous banter with the nurses and staff a
  welcome pleasant distraction.
It's a test of everyone to be sure to get acceptable reaction.
We're all feeling better, despite the reasons we are here,
And I'm sure this progress will continue with the
  optimistic attitude it's clear.
And so in the first instance to get out we wanted to
  shout,
We'll eventually have to force ourselves to say
I'm glad I'm going out.

Reg Morris

THE SCAN

With the wonders of science now known to man,
If you're having a baby you must have a scan.

If you wish to know if it's a son or a daughter,
You'll sit there for hours and drink lots of water.

Lie on your back and apply all this jelly,
Then they run a cold probe all over your belly.

It works by electrics and ultrasound,
They peer in your womb for there it is found.

The object of this is to see it's all right,
You'll get all your photos they're in black and white.

A picture appears on a TV screen,
And your little embryo can now be seen.

You can make out the shape of your little baby,
Curled up and warm in the place it should be.

If it's awake it will turn round,
When it's disturbed by the ultrasound.

You can see its heart beating, make out its nose,
Count all its fingers and tiny toes.

It started out like a little tadpole,
And God only knows how it gets out that hole.

You now know it's here because you can see it,
After nine months you'll want to free it.

Pushing and shoving trying to get out,
But just for now you'll get a print out.

D Wheatley

EMERGENCY ADMISSION

A klaxon pierces in the distance.
The distinctive indigo flashing violently.
The ambulance appears in an instance,
its inmate ushered in silently.

Urgency shows on deadpan faces
as the victim duly arrives
The paramedics go through their paces
fervently hoping the patient survives.

The nurses grasp their acquisition
assessing the damage ever so deftly
issuing demands for requisition,
surmising the situation so swiftly.

A doctor rushes to the scene
beckoned by a nursing student.
He orders treatment by saline
and transfer to intensive care unit.

The atmosphere is so tense
the silence broken by a bleep,
An invisible film of suspense
will he waken from his sleep.

Rebecca Strangward

THE QUESTION

Was Kenneth Clarke
  In the dark
    And Bottomley atrocious?

Or did they see
  Transparently
    And get it all in focus?

Brenda Stockwell

HEAD INJURIES

In the second ambulance

my spells of consciousness last longer.

I'm aware of my accompanying doctor and nurse.
He's at the centre of his experience,
talking away, making her laugh.

The head of A and E: 'Eight days.'
Like a magistrate in pre-First World War
London East End
dishing out a sentence.

I'm under half-hour surveillance:
blood pressure, temperature, pulse,
'move your right arm, move your right leg,
move your left arm, move your left leg,
what's your name?'

Consultant's rounds:
'If you only learn one thing from me this morning -'
Two women in the group: quite separate:
more so than them one small un-English man
who never finds a space to see
what's going on.

Woman in the next bed
claims my alliance.
She doesn't like it here.
She doesn't like the NHS.

No way can I respond
when I'd been two days' monitored
every half hour.

P S Joll

A DEDICATION TO DISTRICT NURSES

It's so many years since a doctor I've seen
I put things off I'm not very keen
I hurt my leg, it worried me so
Then I thought, to the doctor, I will go
He gave me antibiotics, I thought what a curse
Told me I would, next day, be seeing a nurse
These wonderful ladies who are treating me
Always a smile, a chat as well you see
Really, without them, what would we do
They are a Godsend, between me and you
Look forward to seeing them, they're like good friends
I think I'll be sorry when the treatment ends
To these lovely nurses I would like to say
Thank you so much f or your kindness each day
These dedicated ladies, you must feel enchanted.
Sadly to say District Nurses, we take for granted.
'Bless 'em all'

Joan Jeffries

HOSPITAL

Off to the hospital, I did go.
Coughing away, walking slow.
Had an appointment for half past nine
I wasn't feeling all that fine
Sat in the waiting room, looking glum.
Beginning to have pains, in my tum.
The nurse came called my name
I walked in the room with my zimmer frame
The doctor asked, how are you today
I opened my mouth, and started to say.
When in mid-sentence he butted in
To tell me that I was looking thin
I'll send you for X rays to see what's wrong.
Back to the clinic I did go.
Coughing away and walking slow,
Doctor said you need an op.
To get rid of that limp
And that awful cough.

M Alford

WHO AM I?

I work away quickly and quite alone
In a sterile white world, with plates drying,
To help the poorly man with the gall stone,

Or the unseen sweet little child who moans:
The injured, the sick, newborn or dying.
I work away quickly and quite alone,

Surrounded by high technology phones
And red push buttons for magnifying,
To help the poorly man with the gall stone.

Now the laboratory has become my home.
I am conscious of critical timing.
I work away quickly and quite alone.

Family life has been cut right to the bone
So that they can use these sums - these findings -
To help the poorly man with the gall stone.

If I'm more deductive than Sherlock Holmes
I might just help to stop the crying.
I work away quickly and quite alone
To help the poorly man with the gall stone.

Villanelle for a . . .
When I was young it was my only wish
To become a biomedical scientist.

Doreen King

ADMISSION TO HOSPITAL

I came in a hurry
Distressed and afraid
A nurse let me in.
The contents of my handbag
Were poured out on the table.
Each private article
Was tabulated, examined, listed.
I was told to undress
By a doctor.
I stood there naked, vulnerable, afraid and cold.
I was asked to lie
On the examination couch.
The doctor's stethoscope
Was cold on my breast.
She told me to sit up.
She tapped my back,
Tested my reflexes.
Meanwhile two nurses were
Between them
Listing my clothes.
I was told to dress,
And shown into the sitting-room
Where tortured souls
Stared back at me.
I was admitted.

Jenny Cox

NURSE
(Dedicated to my wife)

A nurse trains hard at an early age
and passes the necessary exams.

Gaining practical experience on every ward,
working day and night.

Running each time the buzzer's pushed
and receiving little reward.

From cheering up patients and collecting
bed pans, giving injections and handing out pills.

Lifting and turning patients all day long,
and giving the occasional bed bath.

Giving out food trying to please.

Sisters, Nurses and Doctors rushing about
saving lives, whenever they can.

Time off comes at different times each week.

The job takes all you give,
Satisfaction's your reward.

Three cheers for the NHS.

G F Snook

THE PATIENT'S POEM

Go to the hospital and change your name,
You're called a patient for treatment to gain;
There's doleful looks on the patients' faces
When they go in wards to take their places.

Silence is golden and never a word,
For we trust the surgeon to wield his sword;
He takes out the bad and he leaves the good,
Be obedient as you know you should.

So funny when people have got the bends,
When in hospital they all become friends;
Obey the sister who is always stern,
Take your treatment and you'll make a good turn.

Just find the courage and with faith you come
With forthright effort, the task must be won;
Self silently braced without any word,
The surgeon will work with his trusty sword.

Funny things happen in hospital way,
A compelling hope for a better day;
Thin line of hope is the important word,
The task must be won with the surgeon's sword.

To remember the words that here are said,
Treatment for you in a hospital bed;
Simply a poem, no big words to read,
To prove a hospital is what we need.
Amen.

Dennis Parkes

THE WAITING ROOM

'Next patient for Dr Brown!'
Hunched and glassy-eyed,
Minds and spirits down.

Shuffling, sodden, from the sleet,
Victims of the illness pride
'Next patient for Dr Brown!'

Sick role thespians to a man
Monday's back-ache tide
Models of the tension frown.

Receptionists o' glossy lips,
Thin, sweetly, smiling wide,
'Next patient for Dr Brown!'

The modern scourges of their lives
Fags and booze . . . a downhill slide
And *Stress,* the buzz-word of the town.

An instant cure, or time off work
But effort shall be none
'Next patient for Dr Brown!'
Sufferer from the bright new town.

Ann Ridley

REFLECTIONS OF A HOSPITAL VISIT

How lucky we are.
How we take things for granted.
Having had a few days in hospital it made me realise
How lucky we are.
Whatever our views about the NHS and Trust hospitals
We still must remember how lucky we are
Hospitals are still accessible on demand without checking
your credit rating.

An ambulance is called and you are in.
How lucky we are.
It's only then, you see the vast operation start
To send you out well again
How lucky we are.
Now change things a little.
Say I was not well in a Third World country
What would I be saying then?
They still want me better I know
Although
Where is the hospital, have they got everything
Clean water, disposables, monitoring equipment, medical
back-up, drugs.

The list and questions continue.
My answer remains the same.
How lucky we are.

Stephen Parkinson

NHS PATIENT

I was admitted to hospital
For an operation on my arm.
The day I was admitted,
I was told to sit down and stay calm.
I sat on the bed, and waited patiently
For what seemed hours and hours to me.
In came the nurse, and asked questions galore,
I told her I'd been asked all these before.
It is our duty to get everything right,
After this, you can settle down for the night.
Early next morning, I awoke with a start,
It was only the nurse to check my pulse and my heart.
Two hours later, I was dressed in white cap and socks.
As I was wheeled down to the theatre,
I looked up at the clock.
Half past eight, what a time to go down.
Got to the theatre, there's the doctor in white gown.
He greeted me with a smile, and started to chat
Asking me questions, helping me to relax.
It is the right arm we are operating on, isn't it,
No, it is my left arm . . . just for your benefit.
Everyone laughed, and thought it was funny
I thought, trust me to be so unlucky!
Five hours later, and back in the ward
I said my prayers, and thanked the Lord,
For all the good work these people do.
Just don't know what we would do without them
As they care for me and for you.

E Hinton

THE MENTAL HOSPITAL

Help me from falling in the never-ending trap
From vanity and sanity into easy street's lap;
Where everyone is cushioned from hurt or harm
Yet suffers although life is nothing but calm.

Too late! oblivion! Gates are shut;
They encompass suffering, never heal but
For the residents is guaranteed a life of hell
Until the hospital church sounds the last knell.

Long empty corridors, the occasional nurse
In white linen jacket hurries with a muttered curse,
Heading for the wards hidden even from inside.
Where with needles and cosh injections we abide.

Tuesday is ECT day, everyone looks at the list,
Seeing if they are on 'treatment' the iron fist
Of pentothal which anaesthetises electric shock,
Trolleys clang as bodies revive, doors still have locks.

Graham Lawes

DO YOU RECALL?

Do you recall in days gone by . . .
When nurses' hats seemed to touch the sky,
with starch in their aprons, collars and cuffs.
All pure white, a professional look.
Cottage Hospitals, like small families,
happiness on faces for all to see.
The smell of carbolic, ether and meths . . .

Do you recall in days gone by . . .
Students in sluices, obtaining a shine
on bedpans and trolleys, get rid of the grime.
The ward beds set out in neat little rows,
'Bed baths' and 'Back-rounds' always on the go,
with Doctors and Nurses passing to and fro.
The smell of carbolic, ether and meths . . .

Do you recall in days gone by . . .
When Matron appeared to do her rounds,
the nurses all praying, there's no dust to be found.
Single sex wards, no mixing the two.
No men to see women, that would never do.
Visitors for one hour, but only two to a bed.
The smell of carbolic, ether and meths . . .

Do you recall in days gone by . . .
The patients on bed rest for days on end,
waiting for fractures and scars to mend.
Task allocation, todays jobs to do,
work was hard, but we always got through.
Staff were friendly and never blue.
The smell of carbolic, ether and meths . . .

Patricia A Knight

NEEDS, HOPE AND SENSITIVITY

Some people take life for granted
While others sacrifice their time
They realise others have a need, nursing
People back to health, that's just fine.

A nurse, a care assistant need commending
They've lacked sleep in their day
You might say their our life savers
But with very little pay.

They care for our spirit, they care
For soul and body too
We should be interested, appreciate their
Worth, caring for me and you.

Life is precious, people should come first
Our NHS cannot fail those we as
Nurses, *should nurse.*
Officialdom can cause a lot of
Heartache to the patient.
In part people speak their mind with
A lament.

For myself I've worked with
Young children, and the elderly
Some have been with no sight while
Others with many a disability

These people have cherished
My presence, and tender care.
And I've learned there's hope for
Everyone even through despair.

Spare a thought for our nurses, support
Them where you can
Their our future hope, through whom
We prosper as the common man.

Margaret H Jowsey

ESCAPE

Shrill sirens wail, the doors swing wide
On stretcher case.
A passive form is borne inside
With ashen face.
In rows they wait to learn their fate
With anxious eyes.
Will he decide to operate
Or just prescribe?

What right have I to seek this place
With buoyant tread?
It's plain I show no obvious trace
Of common ill.
It is not I whose heart doth fail
Nor broken bone.
My plaint is but a finger nail
To be wrenched off.

'We'll give you just the slightest puff
To put you out.'
They little thought I'd turn so rough
It took all four
To hold me when I heard one state
In undertone
'That leg is bad, he'll amputate'
Escape I must.

Margaret Nixon

I FELL - WELL THAT'S MY STORY

Crack, I cry out - 'ow.
'Damn and bloody blast it.'
And I throw in another 'ow in for good measure.
An hour gone, my hand is swelling there's pain
And there's a lot of bruising black 'n' blue.

There's the hospital follow the signs for casualty.
Met a nice nurse called Charlie, he looking after me.
Seen the Doctor, she must have been blind
For she asked me what was wrong
And there I was in the cubicle,
Holding my left hand ever so gingerly.

I've heard of follow the yellow brick road,
But I've followed the yellow arrows to x-ray.
I've waited and waited, nearly taken root
Before they took the pictures - twice.
Never once did she ask me to say cheese
And she covered my you-know-whats with a lead blanket.

Seen the doctor - again there's a fracture,
Off to plaster room to have a pot put on.
And what was that she said -
See you next week for fracture clinic.
No, no, *no* - not again.

Ian W Lyon

NO SOAP FOR THE MIDDLEMAN

It's cold in this bed
as cold as their faces
not the nurses
or the doctors
but the suited calculators
loitering like bloody undertakers

They've paid for my misery
by providing coarse blankets
that stink clean
and won't crease
or budge tucked beneath the frame
- we all lie glued the same

The budget pays for nothing
except the bare essentials
of hard pillows
and creaking beds
- they drift about with clipboard flare
watching the covers dying care

If approached and confronted
they'll blame the government
for no help
and no aid
in shifting this parade of distress
though they note it down a success

So when you and I
are laid in their beds
keep one alert eye
on their speeding GTI

Andy McPheat

WARD 31

In a Lancashire town called Ashton,
There Tameside hospital stands.
Nurses of all shapes and sizes,
Some from faraway lands.

Was admitted there some years ago,
Well passed age sixty-five,
A lung complaint called asthma,
It's a wonder I'm alive.

I remember a nurse called Mandy,
All smart in suit of blue,
Always very friendly,
After a shandy or two.

A word about the male staff,
Carl and Martin by name,
A credit to the hospital,
Which stands near the River Tame.

My nebulizer is my loyal friend,
When desperate I must use,
But golden rules I must obey,
No smoking, no women, no booze.

Frank Warren

THE WELFARE STATE

The poverty of a people
Is essentially government's crime,
They espouse their institutions
But who the hell does the time,
They cut back social services
And so-called benefit fraud,
To allocate tax incentives
For the fat-cat's on the board.

Take a look at public healthcare
It's now a standard joke,
With all those private pensions
The national coffer goes broke,
They champion patients' charters
Then stitch up nurses' pay,
While doctors suffer coronaries
Working twenty-four hours a day.

In the interests of the country
They subtly alter facts,
To score political points and
To plaster over the cracks,
But it's really down to a nation
To keep on telling the state,
We really want our welfare
Now, before it's too late.

Michael Gardner

A JOB FOR LIFE

'From the cradle to the grave,'
they had said,
And I had no reason to doubt
their philosophy,
As twenty years ago today I changed from girl to nurse.

Wide-eyed and optimistic
at the start.
Accepting poor pay, long hours -
I had been warned!
Satisfaction nursing people back to health was enough.

Resources were plentiful;
No strikes yet!
Many students on the wards
Made the workload light.
Qualification guaranteed a job for life - I thought.

The Health Service is changing -
Goal posts move.
Technology replaces
Bedside nursing care.
Those who can pay for their treatment are seen most urgently.

As a general practice nurse,
I enjoy
Caring for patients in
The community.
Even here I am not immune from change for change's sake.

So as the millennium
approaches fast.
I must exchange twenty years
Experiences
For a degree in nursing which will make me a better nurse!

Joan Booth

STITCHED UP

I cut my little finger,
It needed one small stitch,
The first time in my honest life
Wished that I was rich.
NHS I'm waiting,
Someone hear my cry,
Nurses with long hours
Rush and pass me by.
Now I'm not one to boast at all,
I never was a moaner,
But put me in the record books
And call me 'King Blood Donor'.
Thank God it's just my finger,
I thought, and then I laughed,
Accidents can't happen
As they're so understaffed.

Paul Deavin

X-RAY VISION

The cubicle measured two by three,
The curtain hid my modesty -
'Undress to nothing and put this on,'
She handed the robe and then was gone.
The dark green gown lay on the chair,
Behind the curtain I now was bare -
Did I wear this garment
Like an overcoat?
A hairdresser's cape?
Or as a cloak?
Feeling hot and confused I wrapped it around -
'Come this way' was the official sound.
A room with equipment - shiny and clean -
'Now stand very still against the screen.'
I stood like a statue
And held my breath -
Another three pictures
Now were done more or less.
I thanked uniformed lady
And gave a weak smile.
Then she spotted my earrings
I'd worn all the while.
Back to the screen,
I had to remain,
Whilst the unsmiling lady
Took my pictures again.

Vanessa A Hulme

NIGHT DUTY

Mrs Boswell wants a bedpan,
Mrs Smithers needs a shot;
Mrs Brown's monopolising
All the patience I've not got.
Mrs Faraday's blood pressure's
Driving mine about sky-high;
Mrs Johnstone is a treasure -
She's just smuggled me a pie!
Mrs Jones thinks it's a favour
Just to pass the time of day;
Mrs Green swears she's in labour,
Though it's still two weeks away.
The ward temperature's sub-tropic,
Though it's snowing hard outside,
And the patients' favourite topic
Is a film I can't abide.
All their constant, draining calls make me
Despair of what I'm worth,
But give it up? Not ****** likely -
It's the greatest job on earth!

Maeveen Clancy

TWO TRIPS TO CASUALTY

I had to go to hospital
I'd had a nasty fall
I'd really hurt my elbow
And it wouldn't move at all
But they said I'd only bruised
Then they sent me on my way
I had to go right back again
And on that very day
They had to take a picture
The nurse was very rude
She said I told you yesterday
That it was only badly bruised
So I went away but still in pain
But I recovered from my fall
It was then four weeks later
That I got a funny call
They said we checked your x-ray
They hadn't noticed at the time
That you had a broken elbow
But by now it should be fine.

Karen Brown

ECONOMY-FRIENDLY SUTURE

Throughout my life's half-century, asthma has raised its ugly head,
More often, than not, putting me on the spot - or, in a hospital bed;
In the early days, intensive care was a steaming, pewter kettle,
Now, it is a steroid course - until the acute symptoms settle.
Crisp, starched uniforms of white, armbands, blue with ruche frill,
Matron's heavy, flat, black shoes, her cutting adjectives shrill,
Yet, decisive, calm, authoritarian, spiced with patient knowledge;
Cremated toast, plastic jam, one lump of cold, grey porridge.

Every morning, doctors' rounds - now, reduced to twice per week,
An endless crowd of juniors, gathers, to take their curious peeks
At obs and ops results, they cluster, closely, around the graphs,
Sleepless nights - the baggy eyes, and over-worked, hollow laughs.
Fresh jug of water, poised, on the locker, to fill a sparkling glass,
Once, the patient's essential right - now, receding task of the past.
Sisters, staffs, auxiliaries, bustling nurses, with paper crowns,
Consistent - though, physical presence is wafer-thin, on the ground.

Ten to fourteen days, interred, was a general course of the cure -
Today, the steroids take command, instant success guaranteed, a sure,
Quick-firing method of filling the patient with energy-laden beans;
Before you are in - you are out, and about, but, what does it mean?
Treating the symptoms is economy-friendly, gives management heart,
But, the ongoing cause - disease - lives, to play a future part
In ravaging the body, spirit and soul - a temporary digression -
Limpid yolk does not cock a snook at the chronically sick's depression.

Christine Baxter

NHS EXPERIENCE

The last time I was in hospital was during a bitter winter storm
And I was gaining the rewards of a previous '9 month horn'
For that was the day my beautiful little baby girl was born
On the NHS

We weren't sure what to expect as the experience was so new
Not a sign of health cuts then and there certainly was no queue
We were given a choice of labour wards and asked which one to choose
On the NHS

We settled in our cubicle and were assigned our own midwife
For what was about to become the happiest day so far of my life
My wife didn't find it quite so enthralling as they had to use a 'knife'
On the NHS

It's only two years since and I now believe the cuts have been quite bad
As you've now to provide your own nappies and your own woman's 'pads'
For them not to give you such basic things it's really got quite sad
On the NHS

The most important thing for authorities now is how to save some cash
We all pay tax and national insurance so we don't want to hear their trash
Managers should give nurses decent money then fix their own financial has
At the NHS

Christopher Leith

NHS . . . OUCH!

Dear Doctor . . . ! Just have this pain,
'Goes down my arm . . . then up again,
He pulled it here . . . Twisted there . . .
. . . Bent my fingers, then gave me
That stare.

'Well my dear,' 'Let me see!'
'I know what's the problem,'
He said, with glec!
'A small jab is needed, that I know,'
'You're suffering from a sore elbow!'

With trembling hand . . . I pulled up my sleeve
. . . Wishing that, I was about to leave.
I stared at the needle, with
Fear and dread . . . as in the distance . . .
. . . The Doctor said,
Those famous words, with his usual wit,
'This little jab, won't hurt a bit!'

After what seemed a lifetime,
I walked through the door . . .
. . . with my poor arm throbbing . . .
. . . much more than before!
Next time I get a similar pain
I will not return to *That Place*
Again!

Pat Drew

INFORMATION

We hope you have enjoyed reading this book - and that you will continue to enjoy it in the coming years.

If you like reading and writing poetry drop us a line, or give us a call, and we'll send you a free information pack.

Write to

Anchor Books Information
1-2 Wainman Road
Woodston
Peterborough
PE2 7BU